ISBN 978-0-483-00177-0
PIBN 10493294

This book is a reproduction of an important historical work. Forgotten Books uses state-of-the-art technology to digitally reconstruct the work, preserving the original format whilst repairing imperfections present in the aged copy. In rare cases, an imperfection in the original, such as a blemish or missing page, may be replicated in our edition. We do, however, repair the vast majority of imperfections successfully; any imperfections that remain are intentionally left to preserve the state of such historical works.

WATSON'S MAGAZINE

Vol. XXIII   JUNE, 1916   No. 2

THOS. E. WATSON, EDITOR

Articles by the Editor

IN THIS NUMBER

Jeffersonian Publishing Co.
THOMSON, :: GEORGIA

The Story of France

Watson's Magazine

Entered as second-class matter January 4, 1911, at the Post Office at Thomson, Georgia,
Under the Act of March 3, 1879.

ONE DOLLAR PER YEAR ▾▾▾ TEN CENTS PER COPY

Vol. XXIII.   JUNE, 1916   No. 2

CONTENTS

Published Monthly by THE JEFFERSONIAN PUBLISHING COMPANY, Thomson, Ga.

Watson's Magazine

THOS. E. WATSON, Editor

Vol. XXIII	JUNE, 1916	No. 2

The Wonderful Career of a Cripple, and the Beautiful Mission Work He's Engaged In.

ONE of our exchanges is a national magazine, named *The Van Leuven Browne.*

Becoming deeply interested in the work described and illustrated in this unique publication, I requested our Managing Editor to write to *The Van Leuven Browne*, requesting the use of the cuts which will be found in this article.

In his reply, he says:

Detroit, Mich., March 18, 1916.
Managing Editor Jeffs.,
    Thomson, Ga.

Dear Madam: Since writing the other letter, I have just thought that it might be expedient to remind you of a few personal affairs. It was the Jefftrsonian that first used the photo of me and my world-famous goat team, in August 1911, accompanied by an article from my pen, which today seems almost prophetic, since I have succeeded in rising in the world's work so rapidly. The year following the appearance of that article, I was elected mayor of the Arkansas city, the next year I became the author of the "Unheard Cry", which book was the first to make its appearance on the subject (I sent Mr. Watson a copy in 1914) then I became established firmly in the work so dear to my heart, and am now, at the age of 24 years, managing editor of this magazine, special writer for twenty-five educational journals, newspapers and magazines, and teacher in the Hospital-School for children and studying the work in every direction with the determination of devoting my life to the national work. A search of your files of August 1911 will give you much information, as well as I remember, which will be proof sufficient of my struggle in getting a start in life, in spite of the fact that I could use but my hand and neither foot. Kindly request Mr. Watson to give full credit of establishing hospital-school and magazine to Miss Browne, the noble little lady who is devoting her life to the cause. I have had nothing to do with the founding of this institution. All the credit is due her in this regard.

Thanking you very kindly for the request and trusting that your magazine will soon carry a ringing plea to the American public on behalf of the crippled child, I am,

Very truly yours,
    JOE F. SULLIVAN.
        Managing Editor.

The following letter is one of those referred to by Mr. Sullivan and it is taken from the file of *The Jeffersonian* for August 1911:

THE MISSION OF THE CRIPPLE.

Dear S. S. B.: As I sit and write this letter, all looks beautiful, smiling and happy this pleasant summer morning; and I feel gratefully fortunate that it has befallen me to experience the constant enjoyment of sweet health, notwithstanding my crippled condition. For if it were not for my good health, I could not enjoy the blessings and beauties that Nature bestows upon me; that is, enjoy them as I do now.

I may look out the north window of my inelegant but closely comfortable little white cottage and see the shining, foam-

gaze out upon this panorama of majestic scenery, which I make common by trying to describe, the thought comes to me that these lucid waters, these richly green banks, these picture-like cataracts, these mighty trees, these deliciously perfumed flowers—all have a mission—a Godly divined and dereed mission, that, however small in comparison with some of God's higher creations, have their allotted part

MRS. BLANCHE VAN LEUVEN BROWNE AND HER YOUNGEST ADOPTED DAUGHTER

ing, rushing Spring River, as it swiftly and noisily rolls down its rocky channel, till at intervals of every few miles it forms little falls or miniature cataracts, which, silhouetted by the sloping, verdant banks and the venerable forests, clothed in a rich drapery of luxuriant leaves and wild flowers, are unsurpassed for natural beauty and picturesqueness.

And as I sit silent and thoughtful and

in the furthering and perfecting of His divine plan.

And as I sit still and think of this interesting subject, a concomitant of the thought expressed above vividly presents itself to me: If these inanimate creations of only one element, matter, have a mission to fulfill during their short and simple existence, why have not we, who are created of three elements, matter, mind and soul, created in His own image, just a little lower than the angels on high, although crippled, deformed and incapacitated?

Can it be that a loving merciful and human may not lend his share of good to humanity and to God? Such would be the condition were it true that the cripples have no mission other than to suffer pain, embarrassment and oftentimes social

JOE F. SULLIVAN

just God gives to His lower creations preeminence over His higher creations, because the higher ones happen to be distorted and disabled from causes beyond direct control? Can it be true that a gnarled but live tree may lend its share of fragrance to the air, and that a deformed ostracism. But thanks to the Almighty, such is not true!

Today I happily celebrate my twentieth birthday. I gladly leave behind me my childhood, my boyhood, my youthhood and am more than willing to take up the duties and burdens of manhood a year earlier than even the laws of my state would allow. Why am I willing and anxious to do such? Because I feel from the depths of my inmost soul that I have a mission in this life; that I have a particular work to do, and that my ambition, so it would seem, is calling me and pleading with me to do that which I believe God would have me to do. As it is with me, so it is with every cripple or invalid, who has life enough and energy enough and ambition enough to realize that he is not a nil (by the will of God) in this world of people.

I may be mistaken when I say there is no one so badly afflicted but that he can do something. But when I read in history of the great and noble men, who blind, crippled, deformed and helpless invalids, and who now, notwithstanding all these handicaps worked diligently and faithfully to do good and to leave to the succeeding generations their names and works as imperishable gifts of God, presented through the hands of man, I am constrained to make my assertion even stronger and broader. I sometimes feel as if I should be correct were I to say that the afflicted, physically, can do more than the strong.

However, I shall not make this assertion, but, instead, I shall say that some of the greatest battles ever fought have been fought by the afflicted, and some of the greatest victories ever won have been won by them. I can say this much and can adduce history to prove it.

Because I am denied the use of my lower limbs for walking and the use of my left arm, it is not sensible or reasonable for any person to say or think that my physical condition, bad as it is, will forever prevent me from supporting myself and helping others in this world. God puts no one here to live purposeless and as a parasite. He has something for us all to do, and with that belief in mind, I will put forth every effort that will tend to transform my unfortunate condition into one whose end will eventually be a blessing.

For instance, Tom Lockhart can use no part of his body save the thumb and forefinger of the right hand; the sight of one eye is entirely gone, that of the other very nearly so; his joints are stiffened and ossified; he has lain in one position more than a quarter of a century, during which time his body has become like a stone statue. Yet this hero of heavenly patience supports himself and nurse by laboriously and painfully scribbling a few lines daily, everyone of which contains a message fraught with the wondrous and infinite love of a suffering, consecrated Christian. He not only provides for himself but makes thousands, who read his writings, happier and more cheerful, thankful and more thoughtful. He has a mission! He is fulfilling it, too!

And the beautiful part of his history is that there are hundreds, similarly and sorely afflicted, who are daily proving that they have work to do and that they are equal to the task of doing it. Yes; we have work to do. And haughty and heartless, and most times dull, is he who says that we are the dross of humanity. For most times we are the purest and the most priceless possessions of Him who, while on earth, graciously knelt by the side of some suffering, neglected invalid or cripple and, gently laying His hand upon him, cured him. He never over-looked them and passed them by. He blessed them and promised them that no suffering and sickness would be known in His Kingdom.

Yes, my silent suffering and nobly patient afflicted ones, when in your melancholy hours the ominously dark clouds of adversity swing low; when the little blue-bells begin mournfully to ring within the walled-up chambers of your pure and consecrated hearts; when your souls begin to pine for the regions where the sun shines bright; when you begin to feel as if you are helpless and worthless to everyone and everything in this old world and that you are unwelcomed burdens to your loved ones; when you very nearly surrender unconditionally to despair, saying you are no account for anything, just turn your pain-marked faces toward the bright side of the house and let the all-sustaining beauties of sweet Hope enter into your sad souls. And then think of the hunch-back Paul; of the stammering Demosthenes; of the blind Milton; of the helpless Pope; of the invalid Stevens; of the blind Helen Keller; of the crippled Will Upshaw, and of hundreds of other afflicted personage of the past and of the present; think of their undying works and of the great good they have done, and are doing, and then say: "I am not worthless; I've been put here for something; maybe to astound the world, but more likely to be humble and to live an exemplary, patient Christian life, and thereby be an inspiration to the struggling, wearied brothers and sisters, who are so strong physially, and yet who are so weak and so easily discouraged. I may be the cause of leading some weary one to his God!"

And as a just hard-earned recompense for your faith and fortitude during this life of pain and confinement, may you one day receive a celestial crown of ineffable glory at the foot of the Great White Throne!   Your friend,

Imboden, Ark.   JOE T. SULLIVAN,

This letter was received and handled by James Lanier, who was at that time the Business Manager of The Jeffersonian Publishing Company. A kind-hearted man, with a great fondness for children and sympathy for the destitute and suffering, he had originated a "Daddy Jim" department in our weekly paper and had developed it into a Home Mission Society, with no frills on it, and no salaried charity-brokers.

We had just celebrated our coming from Atlanta to Thomson, by giving the biggest of barbecues.

It was on the 4th of July, and the

courage and keep going, when suit after suit was being brought against us, and every request for indulgence—on offered partial payments—was refused, none can know save those who were close to me at that unexpected crisis.

Now, consider! Here was an Arkansas boy, a cripple in a little wagon drawn by a goat, arousing the interest of Daddy Jim, and Daddy Jim himself rushing headlong to perdition. A splendidly educated man, who had apparently been round the world and learned something from every place he had visited, a man in the prime of life

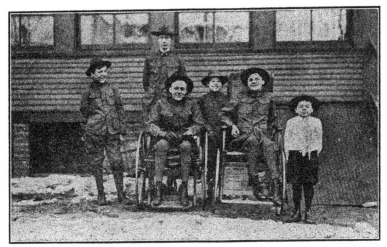

TROOP 5, B. S. A. DETROIT. THE FIRST TROOP OF CRIPPLED BOY SCOUTS IN THE WORLD

crowd was estimated at 10,000—and the cost of the 'cue was about $3,500.

"Daddy Jim" was not present at the plant that day, so far as I know, but was in his office where Mrs. Lytle now works; and, not long afterwards, he asked for a vacation. It was given him, of course, and he went to the mountains of North Carolina.

Naturally, our correspondence then fell into different hands, and we discovered that we were in debt some $25,000, and that ruin was close upon us. Daddy Jim had gone wrong, and we were "up against it."

What a struggle it was to keep up

and in possession of a fine mind and physique, going to the bad, open-eyed, reckless, and yet without any visible or known cause for despair—going down, *down*, and almost pulling us down with him, until one night, far away from here, his uncertain feet take him in front of a railroad locomotive, shifting amid an intracacy of terminal tracks, and poor Daddy Jim's life is ground out.

I am sure from what he said, now and then, when I would mention some rare English book or out-of-the-way episode in English history, that he came of a good family in the Old

Country, that his heart was never anywhere else; and that *somewhere*, in England, there may yet be an old father, or a brother, or a sister who yet expects the return of the restless wanderer, and whose eyes are moist when thinking of "Daddy Jim."

Why have I woven this tragedy into the story of the ambitious, on-going cripple? Because it appeals to me by its contrast, its lesson, a lesson full of inspiration on the one hand and of warning on the other.

road to travel, and that cruel Fate has done them a nasty turn. Too often, they mope over their hard lot, losing precious years in feeling sorry for themselves.

Ah, you Fainthearts! Does it ever occur to you that *you are richer than Rockefeller*, in that *you* don't have to cover your hairless head with a wig, and have a nurse feed you out of a spoon? Does it never dawn upon you that what others have done, you can do?

JAMES AND EFFIE

There are *so* many boys who seem to believe that because they are poor and can't go to college, life has for them no Jacob's ladder reaching to the heaven of success. These mournful and moaning boys have had a good common school education, are in perfect health, are sound in every limb; and yet, because they can't borrow money to go to college, on, they seem disposed to think Jordan a *very hard*

Only a few days ago, the great city of Milwaukee elected a new Mayor, and who do you suppose he was? He was a successful man, of course, but he *had been* a kitchen boy—literally a scullion in the kitchen of a restaurant.

Encouraging as such an example must be to the poor lad at the foot of the hill, think how much more inspiring is the case of Joe Sullivan, the Arkansas cripple. It almost makes me ashamed that I have not done better myself, hard as I have worked since boyhood.

For his motto, this Southern hero takes the lines of Kipling:

And only the Master shall praise us, and
    only the Master shall blame;
And no one shall work for money, and no
    one shall work for fame,
But each for the joy of the working, and
    each in his separate star,
Shall draw the thing as he sees it for the
    God of Things as They Are!

economic and commercial standpoint, dictate this order of precedence, and so Lewis must wait for the hog.

Henry Jones lives in the northeast corner of any Michigan agricultural county, say 20 miles from the county seat. He has, among other stock, a half-dozen pigs. When he goes out to feed them some winter morning he notices that one particular pig, half grown and worth perhaps $5, isn't eating. Mr. Jones goes to his phone and calls the county livestock agent, who got his job from a benevolent legislature through a hog cholera prevention measure passed at the last session.

THESE ARE THE HAPPY KINDERGARTEN CHiLDREN WHO ARE STARTED ON THE ROAD TO HEALTH
!AND INDEPENDANCE AT THE VAN LEUVEN BROWNE HOSPITAL·SCHOOL IN DETROIT

In the April number of the Van Leuven Browne Magazine, are the following headlines and comments:

MONEY FOR A HOG; NONE FOR MERE HUMAN.

Cripple Crawls About in Vain for Aid; but Must Die by Inches—State Which Takes Good Care of Live Stock Has No Resources for Him.

St. Johns, Mich.—Let us consider the case of Henry Jones' hog, and the case of Lewis Wiser.

It is unusual to put the animal first, perhaps; but the United States government and the state of Michigan, from an

The county livestock agent receives $3 a day, mileage, and all expenses, when he works. It's dull on the farm in winter and he is not at all averse to earning a little something. So he drives the 20 miles over to look at Jones' $5 shoat.

If it's really hog cholera he immediately gets busy. There is high-priced serum to buy; maybe part of the herd must be killed. If he is in doubt as to the nature of the disease, he calls in a veterinarian, all without expense to Jones. If the disease baffles the veterinarian, experts are summoned from the Agricultural College at Lansing.

Anyway, they wage a gallant fight for Henry Jones' $5 hog. The expenditure can easily run up to $100. But no matter what it may be, hog cholera must be controlled.

The legislature, made up in large part of farmers and politicians, has said so. And so hog cholera is controlled—and hang the expense.

Now, About the Man.

Having disposed of the important member of the duo under discussion, let us now consider Lews Wiser. The state and the United States rush to the rescue of the $5 hog of Henry Jones, but they haven't much time for Lewis. He isn't good to eat and he didn't have any surgeons over in the legislature fighting for him. The man, maimed and deformed. But he has never lost his capacity for suffering; remember that.

His History.

Lewis Wiser is 31 years old. He was born on a farm in Gratiot county. When he was a small boy his parents moved to a farm of 24 acres near Riverdale, Montcalm county. His people, Mr. and Mrs. Augustus Wiser, are old and feeble. Their little farm barely supports themselves. Wiser is 72 and cannot work much.

In October, 1901, when Lewis was 15 or 16, tuberculosis of the bone appeared in his left leg. The surgeon who ex-

These children are brother and sister, two of a family of three healthy children, stricken with Infantile Paralysis two years ago. They are now perfectly helpless from the waist down. At the Van Leuven Browne Hopital-School in Detroit they will receive an education that will make them independent.

surgeons are busier in the winter than the gentlemen who get sent to Lansing to make laws to safeguard shoats.

And yet Lewis was worth saving—once. What is left of him is worth saving. He has a fine face, a well-shaped head and a high, full forehead. He is willing to work. When you see him you feel that Lewis would have made a useful citizen, a good husband and father. You can imagine that sobered face alight, those hands with the long, slender fingers tossing a chuckling baby in the air. But those things can never be.

For Lewis is a cripple. The state has robbed him of his legs. He crawls pitifully along the ground or rides in a wheelchair. He is but a stump, a morsel of a amined him believed that if he were sent to the University of Michigan hospital for treatment the leg could be saved. He said so, and Lewis wanted to go there. His parents asked that he be sent to Ann Arbor, but they had no money and it was up to the poor authorities of the county.

After considerable delay he was taken to a Big Rapids hospital and stayed there for 12 weeks. His legs had become drawn up by the disease. At Big Rapids, they clipped the cords and tendons. Of course thereafter, if the disease had not progressed, even, he could not have walked.

Disease Progressed.

But it did progress. There were divers operations; a few inches of the bone were clipped off now, and a few inches more six months from now. Finally, in 1908, much too late, he was sent to the Homeopathic hospital and both legs were taken off. Three weeks later, because the flesh would not stay down over the stump, two inches more of bone was taken off his right leg. This completed the sacrifice of his lower limbs.

For five years Lewis lay on a cot; he could not even turn over. But his courage was undaunted. He procured a phonograph and followed the county fairs. He was able to wind the machine and change the records. Those who came a pleasuring threw coins on his cot, if they cared to do so. Many times they didn't because they were in a hurry to get to the race track, where splendidly kept animals worth—oh, many times more than a mere cripple— were performing. Or else they were hastening to the ring where the fat stock, with ribbons on horns, was parading.

Under such circumstances they could be pardoned for not hearing the whine of a cheap phonograph or heeding the cripple who attended it. And yet, sometimes, it must have perplexed Lewis, when he tried to apportion the relative worth of a fast horse or a fat steer—and a mere human being.

Well, Lewis gradually improved. He was able to sit up. When he got a wheel chair and visited various cites of the state selling pencils. He came to St. Johns a year ago to stay at the home of his aunt, Mrs. Charles M. Stanton, and take treatment for Bright's disease at Hart Bros.' hospital. He didn't lose courage at this new affliction, and was getting along until the familiar tubercular symptoms began to appear in his left arm.

Who'll Pay.

"But that meant an operation," said Lewis, gravely, as he sat on the floor and looked up at his questioner, "and operations cost money. I only took in about $100 all last summer, because it rained so much, and I didn't have anything laid up. In fact, I'm a little in debt, but I can get it back next summer if I just have my health. I feel this operation ought to be performed right now."

Lewis believes that if the left arm could be opened and a piece of the diseased bone taken out—three inches of bone were removed from his right arm several years ago and that stopped the progress of the disease in that member—he could go ahead and sell pencils this summer and pay board to his aunt, who needs it, just the same as ever.

Friends of Lewis interested themselves. They know that there are funds for those who cannot take care of themselves. So they went to the poor authorities of Clinton County. There was an investigation. "He hasn't lived here a year yet," said they, "and so under the law, you see, we cannot help him."

"It will soon be a year," Lewis pointed out, "and you could make arrangements for the operation."

"Or stretch a point and perform it now," suggested one of his champions.

"No, no," replied the authorities, "you don't understand. He has been away more or less, so he cannot get legal residence here until he has lived continuously for 12 months in Clinton."

As Lewis must go away each summer to sell pencils, he feels he never will get a legal residence in Clinton county.

It was then suggested that he go over to Lansing and see what could be done. There were any expressions of pity as the legless boy crawled about the capitol corridors and crept from one imposing suite of offices to another. But pity hasn't alleviated the ache in that arm.

Well, What Now?

"They told me that the sanatorium for consumptives in Howell was full," said Lewis, two lines of puzzlement deep between his eyes. "In the state board of health I said I understood there was a fund for taking care of fellows like me. The doctor in there—I used to see him at Big Rapids—he said there was such a fund, but—well, I couldn't just understand him. I think he said it was all used for experimentation. My arm was hurting pretty bad. I went from one place to another as they told me to do, but no one seemed to know. Oh, yes, I guess they cared, but they couldn't seem to do anything."

"Well, what now, Lewis?"

"The Clinton poor board has written to Montcalm County. They say over there they will treat me at the poorhouse if I go back. But I don't want to go to the poorhouse. I'm not a pauper. I can take care of myself if they'll only fix me up. Besides, I remember what they did before —the cheap thing, and not the best thing. I want to have treatment at the hospital here or else at Ann Arbor."

Unreasonable? Of course! A tubercular patient without money has no right to likes and dislikes and a decent pride. And yet—and yet, you recall they didn't make Henry Jones' pig go to the county seat when they suspected he had hog cholera!—Detroit News.

Even now the Southern Baptist Churches are threshing the waters into a foam, because the charity-brokers want a Million Dollar Judson Memorial fund—for what?

They say themselves that they intend to spend the Million Dollars in building more Hospitals and Colleges for the heathen, in China, India, Japan, and other lands into which missionaries go for health, pleasure, easy-life and big salaries.

The other churches are just as crazy: they can see a sore on the hind-leg of a Chinaman, in China, better than they can see a cancer on the face

School which she established twelve years later in a rented house, with borrowed furniture, and one child. Her work has grown in efficiency and has accomplished such remarkable results in cases which were supposed to be incurable that the Hospital-School now stands among the foremost of America's institutions for the care of crippled children.

Miss Browne developed her idea of a service to cripples, and with the support of her Board of Trustees has successfully and conclusively proved the correctness of

BOY SCOUTS AT THE VAN LEUVEN BROWN HOSPITAL-SCHOOL, DETROIT

of a Southerner, in the South. They are clamorously bent on donating free education to the children of Orientals, and determined that the parents here at home shall be taxed by the State and robbed by the School-book Trust, if *their* children get any mental uplift.

In contrast with the Memorial builders of Hospitals and Colleges in China—on American money—consider this home mission:

The Van Leuven Browne Hospital-School for crippled children was founded in Detroit in June, 1907, by Miss Blanche Van Leuven Browne, herself a cripple, Miss Browne was a patient for a year in St. Luke's Hospital, Chicago, and it was at this time, when fifteen years of age, that she conceived the idea of a Hospital-

her theory, both as to physical and mental training for crippled children.

Of one hundred and eighty-three children received as incurable at the institution, 14 per cent. have been absolutely cured and 50 per cent. have been greatly benefited physically and mentally. Underlying the work of the institution and in a measure distinguishing it, have been two recognized facts—first, in order to make cripples independent and self-supporting, special mental training as an offset to physical disability is necessary; and second, that most cripples have mental capacity susceptible of development to an unusual degree, all they need is opportunity. The Hospital-School has attempted—and with marvelous success—to furnish this opportunity.

Miss Brownie has given gladly, cheerfully and untiringly of her best efforts in all branches of the work, personally superintending every department and directing the raising of funds for maintaining it as well.

It is now planned to build an Educational Colony for cripples on a forty-acre tract near Detroit. It will be the first colony of its kind in the United States, and $50,000 was raised in December for the purpose of establishing it. The Colony will consist of cottages, each cottage to be

hotel to accommodate visitors to the Colony.

The cost of establishing the Colony is estimated at $200,000, proportioned approximately as follows:

40 acres of ground............$	10,000
Graded School................	6,000
Administration Building........	6,000
Industrial Training School......	6,000

MILDRED QUINN

built as the home for twelve children, a nurse and a maid. There will be a graded school, a manual training school and an isolation hospital in the Colony. The administration building will be centrally located; all buildings will be connected by cement walks and there will be no thresholds. All buildings, except the administration building, will be one story; the second floor of the administration building will be fitted up as a small

Isolation Hospital..............	10,000
Eight cottages ($6,000 each)....	48,000
Eqipment and maintenance of Colony and Kenilworth Avenue Receiving Home and Hospital for one year...........	12,000
	$100,000
Endowment	100,000
	$200,000

The Van Leuven Browne Hospital-School is a perpetual Charity for the benefit of crippled children.

It was established June 22, 1907, in five rooms with borrowed furniture and one child.

It does 75 per cent. charity work.

It has a present registration of 30 pupils. It has the only Boy Scout organization and Camp Fire Girls' organization

made up of men and women of standing in the community. It is maintained by voluntary contributions.

All services rendered to the Hospital-School and all moneys, bequests, legacies and donations received by the School are expended to alleviate the sufferings of chronically diseased children.

All property titles are held in the name

TWO CHILDREN SAVED BY THE VAN LEUVEN BROWNE HOSPITAL-SCHOOL

zation and Camp Fire Girls' organization of crippled children in the world.

Its average yearly maintenance expense is $7,900. This amount provides a cheerful, pleasant home, the best surgical and medical treatment obtainable, schooling and industrial training for 30 children.

It is a Home, a Training School and Hospital where any physician of good standing may send his patients and have his instructions for each case carried out.

It is managed by a Board of Trustees

of the Board of Trustees of the Van Leuven-Browne Hospital-School. All expenditures are governed by the Board of Trustees. All books are audited by Public Accountants.

Experienced nurses and teachers are employed and the children respond wonderfully to the treatment, training and education. Many cases considered quite hopeless have been cured in the eight and a half years since the Hospital-School has been established.

Seventy cents per day covers the cost of the care of each child, demonstrating careful and economical management.

Its object is to provide a Hospital, School and Home combined, for the treatment, education and training of crippled children and those with chronic diseases; to aid them to become at least partially self-supporting by means of education and the careful training of any special talent a child may have.

It is absolutely non-sectarian, its children are Protestant, Catholic, Jewish; some of them come from homes of no religion.

It is open to all crippled white children who need its care.

Children who cannot pay are received absolutely free.

Recently, Mr. Sullivan has published a folder containing messages of encouragement sent him in years gone by. Among these he cherishes the following:

Elbert Hubbard—
"Things are coming your way."
Fred Heiskell, Managing Editor Arkansas Gazette—
"You are fighting in a good cause and I should like to help you."
The Supt. Public Instruction of Michigan—
"I want a sketch of your life and labor to be used in boys' work in the state."
Alice Louise Lytle, Managing Editor Watson's Magazine—
"I want to use you for an illustration of what a man of misfortune can do, if he makes up his mind."
Gilbert D Raine, Publisher Memphis News Scimitar—
"I have paid hundreds of dollars for stuff that was not worth as much to the News Scimitar readers as your last article."
Congressman W. A. Oldfield—
"Inclosed herewith I hand you a clipping from the magazine section of the New York World, which shows that your fame is spreading. I congratulate you."

On the message from our Mrs. Lytle, he margins the question—"Do you remember writing me this? It was just before you went to Florida for your health."

A few days ago Dr. Nicholas Murray Butler, of Columbia University, New York, amazed and disgusted all right-thinking people by eulogizing the traitor and assassin who over-

threw the government of Mexico, and plunged his country into the revolution which has raged ever since. Dr. Butler severely arraigned Presidents Taft and Wilson for not becoming moral accomplices after the fact in that horrible murder of Madero, by accepting the bloody hand of Huerta and giving him the support of this Government.

Mr. Sullivan re-prints another of Dr. Butler's cynical speeches, not less grossly immoral and unprincipled than his praise of Huerta:

"Educate only the fit," says Dr. Nichols Murray Butler, president of Columbia University, and college presidents all over the country echo his sentiments. They reason from a standpoint of economics that it is a waste of time, effort and money to put the facilities of the colleges at the disposal of the physically weak."—The New York American.

Staggering verbal blows often fall from the lips of intellectual giants just as terrific physical blows come from the fists of pugilists. The assertion on education, quoted above and taken from a recent issue of the New York American, is less staggering or startling, probably, because of its source, as it seems that this particular university is manned by a crowd of learned professors who make a specialty of getting into the limelight.

"Educate only the fit." That statement must stand upon the strength of its own merits. But the concomitant thought is, Who are the unfit? Education is the art of developing the intellectual and moral faculties of man. Therefore, if education is mental development, he who is "unfit" is he whose mind is not capable of being developed. Thus the "unfit" are the idiots, imbeciles and feeble-minded, and not those who through misfortune have been deprived of physical perfection. On the other hand, if one should say that a certain person was fit for an athlete he would mean that the person was particularly fit on account of his physical strength. A "weakling" is an "unfit" in athletic circles.

As everybody knows, the English poet, Alexander Pope was physically unfit, from a child. Each morning his clothes had to be put on him, and it was necessary to stitch them tightly to hold him up.

William of Orange, King of England, was an invalid all his life; but he beat the proud Louis the Grand, King of France, drove the Stuarts and their Jesuits out of England, and gave them a finishing blow at the Battle of the Boyne.

An Englishman born blind, became Postmaster General of the greatest empire on earth; and the greatest of French historians cried out one day, in the torture of his utter physical helplessness and agony, "O that I were *only* blind!"

Among the world's famous men, thinkers and doers, there were many that had no such physique as that of the self-complacent Dr. Nicholus Murray Butler—who writes his name in full to prevent his identity from being merged into the common herd of Butlers—but those unfortunately deformed men helped very much to make the worldly arrangements and conditions amid which lives and thrives such commonplace models of corporeal perfection as Dr. Nicholas Murray Butler.

Tamerlane was a cripple, and had been exposed to die, as not "fit": Mahomet was an epileptic, from childhood: Demosthenes was a consumptive stammerer: Talleyrand's parents practically abandoned him because he was a cripple: Richard Brinsley Sheridan was pronounced a hopeless dullard, when a school-boy: and scores of the most dynamic authors, statesmen, inventors, scientists, philosophers, and generals were physically unfit, from their very cradles.

Alexander H. Stephens, always feeble, never mellowed, broadened, and did his best work until he became so physically helpless that his body-servant had to bathe him, dress him, and treat him like a child.

Perhaps, the greatest statesman France has ever known was Richelieu; and *he* also, was physically unfit, not even able to sit a horse, and he had to lie down in a litter when he was on a journey.

None but the most superficial of observers would ever condemn a child, as not fit to educate, because of physical malformation. On the contrary, some theorists have held that there is a mysterious kinship between genius and disease, just as there is an nuquestionable relation between religious emotion and sexual excitement. God alone could explain such things.

My hero, Mr. Sullivan asks some questions, and you might think about them, whether you can answer them or not:

1. How many Crippled Children live in your city, or county or state?

2. How many attend school, or how many are out of school because of physical or financial inability to attend? (Only two State Superintendents of Public Instruction in the United States could answer that question January 1, 1915.)

3. Did you ever see a school or college for Cripples, maintained by the State, as those for the Deaf, Dumb and Blind?

4. Did you ever see the Church provide for the education of the Cripples as it does for the Heathen at a cost of nearly $100,000,000 annually?

5. Did you ever hear of a minister making an effort to provide a conveyance for a Crippled Child to attend Sunday School or Church?

6. Do you not .believe that a Crippled Child is as valuable to God and to humanity as the Heathen?

7. Did you know that your State Constitution says that all children of mental power shall have an opportunity to receive an education and that money is collected as taxes for that purpose?

8. And did you know that the Crippled Children are robbed annually of their pro rata of this school tax?

9. Did you know that there are 250,-000 Crippled Children in the United States and that fewer than 5,000 were in school last year.

10. Is that a fair ratio?

11. Did you know that there are more than 100 Schools and Colleges in this country, maintained by State, Church and Societies, for the Deaf, Dumb and Blind, and that there are not as many thus afflicted persons combined as there are crippled and incapacitated physically?

12. Isn't there something wrong in this sort of business?

13. Did you know that only four states have seen the necessity of an educational system for the Crippled Child and that there is not even a class .for Cripples in any of the Southern or estern States?

14. Did you know that there was the sum of $700,000,000 expended in this Na-

tion last year for education, with an additional $100,000,000 for the care of feeble minded?

15. And did you know that Chicago spent about $30,000 for Crippled Children, with New York slightly in the lead? Is that a fair ratio?

16. Did you know that the Spartans used to condemn every imperfect child to death?

17. Did you know that Civilization in America has condemned nearly every Cripple to a mental darkness worse than death by denying him his inalienable right to an education that will provide a means of support?

18. Did you know that every crippled or deformed child in America is virtually an alien in the sight of those who enforce the educational laws?

19. Did you know that Germany, England, Italy, Norway, Sweden and several other European countries educate every Crippled Child to the degree that it is self supporting?

20. Don't you believe you owe it to your fellow-man and to Humanity to investigate this matter and ascertain the true condition?

The Privilege

Ralph M. Thomson.

We may not gain the mountain top,
    The distant goal we glimpse afar,
Where heaven seems about to drop
    Upon the towering peak a star—

We may not reach the beckoning crest,
    That wears the halo of the sun,
Where blue-eyed Nature smiles her best,
    And earth and sky appear as one;

But we, comrade, by day and night,
    Come weal or woe at Fate's command,
At least, in struggling toward the height,
    May walk life's valley hand-in-hand.

Erasmus, the Most Polished Scholar that Ever Belonged to the Roman Church

FROM time to time, I have quoted in this magazine the terrible accusations made by Erasmus against the secret societies of his church, against the vices and crimes of convents and monasteries, and against the mercenary paganism which he regarded with horror, and against which he appealed to the Pope.

Of course, the Romanists have been embarrassed by having an illustrous Catholic scholar placed in evidence against the sottish priests who rule American papists.

The average priest, nowadays, is so utterly ignorant, so incased in arrogance, and so impervious to common sense, and so brutally intolerant, that he is unable to concede that any assailant of the degeneracy of his church can be honest, or that any mountain of evidence, as to the corruption of monastic institutions, could ever have been veritable mole-hills.

In short, the American priest is more rabidly papal than many of the Popes have been; and his narrow mind divides the human race into two classes, the Blessed and the Damned—the Blessed being Romanists who blink at no monstrosity of the popish system, and the Damned being those who, having eyes, *see;* and who, having seen, will speak out against wrong, although the wrong be precious to the papal heart, because it is a mechanical cog in the great iron wheel of pagan-papal Romanism.

This mental attitude of the American Catholics—who are more ultramontane than the European fanatics—is finely illustrated by an approved article in *Truth,* the New York magazine of The American Catholic Truth Society.

The text of the writer and his excuse for slandering the most brilliant reputation of literary Catholicism, is thus worded—

"In the December issue of a popular magazine, there appeared a laudatory reference to *The Praise of Folly,* by Erasmus."

That's the text, that the excuse, that the provocation: now read the libellous arraignment of the honored dead Catholic, by a living Catholic who is both bigot and ignoramus:

Who, let us ask, is this Erasmus, and what are we to think of him? Luther calls him "a septice and an epicurean." Joseph Sauer, in the Catholic Encyclopedia, says of him: "His vanity and egotism were boundless, and to gratify them he was ready to pursue his former friends with defamations and invective; his flattery, where favor and material advantages were to be had, was often repulsive, and he lacked straightforward speech and decision in just the moments when both were necessary. His bitter sarcasm had done much to prepare the way for the Reformation. It spared neither the most sacred elements of religion, nor his former friends. He was unable to grasp firmly ecclesiastical doctrine or deal justly with scholastic formation, while, on the other hand, he inveighed with extreme injustice against the institutions of the Church."

In his "Colloquia," the tone and the language are so offensive that even Luther, in his "Table Talk," declares: "If I die I will forbid my children to read his 'Colloquies.'" The Papal Legate, in his reports to Rome, said of hime: "The poison of Erasmus has a much more dangerous effect than that of Luther." Erasmus resembles the modernist of our own days. Whilst he vilified the Church he wished at the same time to remain within her fold. His "Praise of Folly," says Sauer, "is a cold-blooded, deliberate attempt to discredit the Church." That his thoughts were not her thoughts his writings sufficiently show. In order to know rightly what we ought to hold in the Church militant, St. Ignatius of Loyola lays down that the following rules are to be our guides. First, laying aside all private judgment, we ought to keep our minds prepared and ready to obey in all things the true Spouse of Christ Our Lord, which is Our Holy Mother, the Hierarchial Church. The second is to praise Confession made to a priest, and the reception of the Most Blessed Sacrament once a year, and, what is, better, once a month, and, still better, every eight days always with the requisite and fitting dispositions. The third is to praise the frequent hearing of Mass, also hymns, psalms, and long prayers, both in and out of the church, and likewise the hours ordained at fixed times for the Divine Office, for prayers of any kind, and for the Canonical hours. The fourth is to praise greatly religious orders, and a life of virginity and continency, and not to praise the married state as much as any of these. The fifth is to praise the vows of religion, of obedience, poverty, and chastity, and vows to perform other works of perfection and supererogation. The sixth is to praise the relics of saints, showing veneration to the relics, and praying to the saints and to praise likewise the stations, pilgrimages, indulgencies, jubilees, and candles lighted in churches. Seventh is to praise the precepts with regard to fasts and abstinences, as those of Lent, Ember Days, Virgils, Fridays and Saturdays; likewise not only interior, but exterior penances. The eighth is to praise the construction and the ornaments of churches, and also the veneration of images, according to what they represent. Finally to praise all the precepts of the Church, keeping our minds ready to seek reasons to defend, never to impugn them.

Bitterly, he arraigns Erasmus, because the profound student of the Bible —and translator of the New Testament —scouted prayers to saints as a recent innovation, not supported by Scripture; because he ridiculed beads, as an imposition upon the ignorant; because he scornfully repudiated the idea that priests and popes can forgive sins; because he roundly denounced the priests as deluders of the people; and because he spoke of the sale of "indulgences" as a cheat and swindle. Finally, this American traducer of the great Dutch scholar declares, that he was worthless in character, and was not to be credited; and he quotes the malignant words of one Baudrillart who said of Erasmus, "*Though a religious, he abandoned his convent.*" As every well-read literary man knows, *the Pope released Erasmus from his conventual vows;* treated him ever with the most honorable attention;

wrote him personal letters; persuaded him to take up his wonderful pen against Luther; *and offered to make him a cardinal!*

The modest scholar excused himself from becoming the Pope's guest at the Vatican, but yielded to the request to combat the doctrines of Luther, declining the proffer of the cardinalate, upon the grounds of his health, his literary habits, and his lack of wealth.

Honorable to the Pope to offer it; honorable to the famous scholar to decline it.

What is your opinion of the sincerity of an American Catholic who can defile the pages of a Romanist magazine with such a libellous account of a great Catholic of the 16th century who was *the favored friend of three Popes?* What is your opinion of the editorial capacity of a magazine which will publish that kind of virulent defamation?

Either those who give this kind of wicked misrepresentation to their Catholic readers are deliberately malevolent, or they are ludicrously ignorant. In either case, it is a deplorable circumstance, that American Catholics have to look to such sources for information.

In the hope that the subject may be of interest to you, I will endeavor to condense in briefest form the facts which will picture to your mind this marvellous Dutchman, friend of the most powerful men of his day, esteemed by Sir Thomas More, respected by King Henry VIII., flattered by the Emperor Charles V., courted by King Francis I., welcomed in the castles of the noble, and signally indulged by Popes Julius II., Paul II., and by Leo X., *who gave his personal sanction to the learned man's classic translation into Greek of the very incorrect Latin Vulgate of Jerome.*

"There is a musty chronicle, written in tolerable Latin, and in it a chapter where every sentence holds a fact. Here is told with harsh brevity the strange history of a pair who lived untrumpeted, and died unsung, four hundred years ago, and lie now as unpitied in that stern page as fossils in a rock. Thus, living or dead, Fate is still unjust to them; for if I can but show you what lies beneath that dry chronicler's words, methinks you will correct that indifference of centuries, and give those two sore tried souls a place in your heart—for a day."

With this deft and feeling touch, Charles Reade begins his fascinating story of *The Cloister and the Hearth*, wherein the lives of Gerard and Margaret, "those two sore tried souls," run their troubled, tragic, changing course through the wide panorama of the 15th century—a panorama sketched with masterly hand, picturing the customs, manners, superstitions, and conditions of an era in which a man's life was the property of the feudal lord, and his soul, the plaything of the Roman priest.

Gerard and Margaret (the one a son of a merchant of Tergou, and the other, a daughter of a physican of Sevenbergen) lived in Holland towns, not far apart; and they loved each other with the too-eager passion which has caused so many scalding tears, so many wild deeds, so many broken hearts. Betrothed, formally and in church, they were not wedded, before the ardor of youth drew the element of tragedy into their lives.

Gerard must needs go to Rome, while Margaret remains at Sevenbergen; and wicked marplots intercept their letters in the old way of the wicked. Word comes to Gerard that Margaret is dead; and in the agony of his incurable wound, he is artfully worked upon, in Rome's old artful way, and he is persuaded to take the vows of priesthood.

But Margaret is not dead, only bowed down with the burden of desolation and apparent desertion, in the midst of which she gives birth to a child, who, after a trying ordeal of his own, will rise upon the admiring gaze of the world as the brightest, wittiest, most honest, and most thorough literary genius of his time.

If you would learn what were the conditions—mental, social, political, moral, and religious—of the 15th century; and if you would care to follow out, to the end, the lives of Gerard and Margaret, read *The Cloister and the Hearth:* as for me, I must take up the story of the illegitimate boy, who rose from humble station and discouraging beginnings, to the supreme light of European letters.

The historian, Froude, gives the year 1467 as the year of the birth of Erasmus, and Rotterdam, as the place. He also mentions the fact that the boy inherited a small property which his guardians either embezzled, or lost by mismanagement.

At the age of fifteen, the lad had shown a wonderful fondness for reading, and had begun to compose poems, essays, &c., after the manner of all precocious boys; hence, he had attracted the attention of the monks, who urged him to take the customary perpetual vows.

It was against the laws of the church, *then*, for such vows to be taken, before majority; and it ought to be a felony, *now*, for priests to inveigle boys and girls into thus taking upon themselves slavery for life; but even in the 15th century the monks were so eager and unscrupulous, that King Henry IV., of England—who owed his throne to a Catholic intrigue against the Plantagenet rightful heirs—felt constrained to have his Parliament severely condemn the practise of kidnapping boys and girls into convents and monasteries.

After a vain struggle, the orphan boy, Erasmus, yielded partly to persuasion, partly to fraud, and partly to the force of necessity; and so, at the age of seventeen, this delicate, dispeptic, fastidious youth, was made to take the irrevocable vows to a monastic life, in the order of Augustinian monks.

The experiment was almost fatal to the victim: Erasmus languished, and fell into so wretched a condition of forlorn unhappiness, that the prior of the monastery took pity on him. The prior could do nothing himself, but advised the boy to appeal to the Bishop of Cambray. This was done, probably in person, by Erasmus; and the Bishop, a man of kindness, agreed to take the youth into his palace, as his secretary. So narrow as this, was the escape of the book-loving lad, from the pestilential dung-heap of a 15th century convent.

The Bishop, from time to time, allowed Erasmus to study at Louvain, one of the very few Catholic cities, where a very few favored young men could obtain the semblance of an education.

In 1492, Erasmus became an ordained priest, and the Bishop gave him leave to visit Paris, for the purpose of attending the university there; and the prelate made the ambitious young man a small allowance for his support, while pursuing his studies.

In the gay French capital, Erasmus was eagerly welcomed, for his reputation as a scholar had gone on ahead of him, some of his poems had been circulated, and his delightful conversational gifts captivated those with whom he mingled.

Not being able to maintain himself on the Bishop's allowance, he took in pupils, who came to him to learn Greek.

At Paris he made the acquaintance of some young English noblemen, who became his warm friends; and, at their instance, he visited England, where he was given a splendid reception, being presented at court, and entertained at Oxford.

It was at this time that he came to personally know the prince who was afterwards Henry VIII., a name detestable to *papists*, but not to *Catholics*, for Henry never ceased to be a most devout, exacting, blood-shedding Catholic, himself.

Erasmus, not much later, published his first book, called *Adagia*, and made up of anecdotes, witticisms, proverbs, quotations, popular sayings, and any other amusing thing that came to hand. In the *Adagia*, the monks, friars, and priests fared badly; but everybody laughed, enjoyed the book, and spread the fame of the author.

Archbishop Warham read *Adagia* with delight, and offered Erasmus a benefice, if he would settle in England. However, the thirst for knowledge

was unsatisfied, libraries were few, and far apart; and so we find the restless student going to Antwerp, to read the books collected there. What a commentary upon the absurd present-day assertions of Romanist partisans, that there were never any Dark Ages; and that Catholic Europe, in the middle period, was studded with universities, at which throngs of young folks lapped up learning.

That type of partisan is even willing to paint you a vivid mental picture, *of a Catholic lay-world*, flowing with the milk and honey of vernacular Bibles, which peasants, commoners, and aristocrats perused, eagerly, in the sweet and secure privacy of the hearthstone, where liberty of conscience and freedom of worship were as familiar and tolerated as household cats.

Erasmus found it different: the universities of all Europe did not number a dozen: the few books were chained to the shelves of the widely scattered libraries; classic manuscripts—which were beginning to be imported from the Mohammedan East to take the place of those burned by Popes and besotted monks—were jealously guarded.

Although pensioned by the Bishop of Cambray, and patronized by the Archbishop of Canterbury, the brilliant Erasmus found it a task of enormous difficulty to acquire, in several capitals and scores of monasteries, the knowledge which now makes one small department of any well-selected library. If this was true of so favored, famous, and popular a young *priest*, what must have been the obstacles blocking the way of the ordinary *layman?*

As Erasmus developed intellectually, and became more and more a master of classic literature, one predominating idea took possession of him, namely; *that popery had become almost the same as ancient paganism.*

The machinery of the one system had been modelled upon that of the other: the superstitions of both systems were the same in substance, even when different in name: the tyranny, the greed, and the corruption of the olden system had reproduced themselves in the new;

and the modern paganism was the more baleful to the world, in that it terrorized the brains of men, and shed their blood, most ferociously, *on mere differences of opinion*, concerning matters about which there could not possibly be positive proof, and which not only denied the evidence of one's own eyes, but the dictates of one's common sense.

Defying the hidden truths of the Scriptures—*for no layman and few priests ever read the Book*—the modern paganism challenged human reason, placing upon the mind of man a burden too monstrous for national endurance; and (as if maddened by the pagan gods who meant their destruction) the Popes, the Cardinals, the Bishops, the monks, the friars, and the priests, made Europe ring with the scandal of their ungodly, indecent living.

In vain had the dauntless Florentine Catholic, Savonarola, lashed the vices and the crimes of his church, with the scorpions of his fiery tongue: the answer of the wickedest of all modern Popes had been, *to burn the would-be reformer.*

But the Catholic world was troubled: Eastern books were entering Europe: a wrathful revolt against childish monklore, monk-education, and monk-lies about "Saints," was gaining a foothold among the upper classes: teachers from Constantinople were brought into Italian cities to found schools of classic learning: seeds of Wycliffism and French skepticism began to germinate and bear fruit: the secret orders of monks and friars had grown so powerful and so arrogant, that the regular clergy were angrily jealous, while the Vatican itself became alarmed.

Thus, a number of circumstances, operating together, *threw discord into the ranks of the clergy, and compelled the Popes to be passive.*

This is the true reason why Erasmus was able to write so freely against the usurpations, the superstitions, and the crimes of the papal system.

Conditions were not favorable for another Huss and Jerome atrocity; nor was Erasmus a man whom the temporal princes would have permitted the church to murder, *for telling the truth,*

Therefore, the chaste and learned Dutchman could publish his *Praise of Folly*, his *Colloquies*, and his Greek translation of the New Testament, filling the latter with marginal notes, horribly "heretical," any one of which notes would have caused the Pope's own Inquisition at Rome to torture and kill him, in the good old days when Pope Alexander VI. caused Savonarola to be burned.

Erasmus did not hesitate to describe the monks as sots, dolts, impostors, cheats, swindlers, and "hooded whoremongers." The entire monastic system came under his sweeping condemnation. All the fire of his nature was aflame, when he spoke of the enticement of immature boys and emotional girls into lifelong servitude, behind the walls which hid every abuse, and shut off all hope of escape.

He boldly blamed the church for making it an unpardonable sin for priests to marry, and yet easily tolerating their debaucheries and their notorious concubinage.

In fact, Erasmus arraigned the entire un-Scriptural papal system, scathingly:

"Obedience is so taught, *as to hide that there is any obedience to God.* Kings are to obey the Pope. Priests are to obey their bishops. Monks are to obey their abbots.

Oaths are exacted, that disobedience may be punished as perjury.

It may happen, and often does happen, that an abbot is a fool or a drunkard. He issues an order to the brotherhood in the name of holy obedience. And what will such order be? An order to be chaste? An order to be sober? An order to tell no lies?

Not one of *these* things!

It will be, that a brother is not to learn Greek; *he is not to educate himself.*

He may be a sot. He may go with prostitutes. He may be full of hatred and malice. He may never look inside the Bible.

No matter. He has not broken any oath. He is an excellent member of the community.

But if he disobeys such a command (as not to study and instruct himself), there is the stake or dungeon for him, instantly."

No wonder that the monks raved against Erasmus, and demanded his return to prison, the monastery. *"Dickey bird, Dick bird, come and be killed"* they sang, with insistent chorus, but the song did not compel the canny Dutchman. Erasmus loved life; and he had no desire whatever to be throttled by brutal monks, and walled up inside the bricks.

Nobody knew better than he what would happen, if he ever allowed the monastic dungeon to close its doors on *him,* again.

Happily free, he remained free, and no urgency of pressing invitations from those who reminded him of his vows could prevail upon him to go and get himself canonically murdered.

His *Praise of Folly* had immense popularity: nearly every European who could read, revelled in the literary luxury afforded by this marvellous book.

The breath of eternal life is in it, for it expresses the piety of a sincere believer in the meek, merciful, and charitable Christ, as distinguished from the fanatical fury of a man-killing bigot, the grovelling humility of a priest-ridden imbecile, or the self-righteous arrogance of a better-than-thou pharisee: and it will ever remain the most scholarly, unanswerable, and nobly-meant indictment of the paganism which the Roman bishops and theologians had introduced into the Christian religion, to the utter eclipse of New Testament gospel.

Montaigne had jeered, and sneered, and adroitly undermined popery; but Montaigne had not published his "Essays," and the worldly French skeptic not only remained a good Catholic, but went to Rome and kissed the Papa's foot.

Rabelais had poured his broadsides into the system of Rome, which he had seen from within; but Rabelais had been obliged to save his own body from the stake by covering the greater part of his meaning—so that the success of his book was literary, rather than revolutionary.

But in Erasmus, the world recognized a dynamic force, whose purpose could not be misunderstood, and whose voice could not be hushed. His orthodoxy could be established by the Gospels, and by The Fathers of the early church. His motives could not be questioned, for he had not accepted the highest offices when his church offered them to him, nor had he left the fold.

Consequently, he was neither heretic nor rebel: he was nothing more—and nothing less—than a scholar living by his pen, a Christian content with his lot, the celebrity of literary Europe; and all that he asked of Popes and prelates was, *a reform of crying abuses in the church.*

Summed up in simple terms, the meaning of the books of Erasmus was:

"Return to the doctrines and the formation of the primitive church: make the broad, humane, and purifying lesson of Christ, *yours:* do not kill fellow Christians because they cannot believe, in all things, as you do: abolish convents and monasteries: permit the priests to take wives, instead of concubines: drive out of the Temple the mercenary monks, and indulgence-sellers who have defiled it: don't pretend to usurp God's power to forgive sins: cast out your saint-worship, and your adoration of idols and images: be Christ-like in living, and do not deceive yourselves by thinking that lust, greed, pride, ambition, intolerance and murderous tyranny can ever be accepted among sane people, *as Christianity.*"

You can see well enough why the papists of the present day, dread the influence of Erasmus, and forbid the reading of his books: he was a Scriptural Christian, *heart and soul.*

He was a disciple of the old school; a believer who might have *exhorted,* after Paul *preached,* on the hill of Mars. He was an Apollos who fain would have *watered,* what Paul had *planted.*

The papists gnashed their teeth at him *then,* and they have been industriously keeping it up, these four hundred years, thus proving how rancorously they can hate even a Catholic, *if that Catholic reads, and is guided by, the New Testament.*

In contrast to the scurrilous estimate of Erasmus, written for and endorsed by Senator Randell's *Truth* magazine, let me reproduce a letter written by the Catholic monarch, Charles V., Emperor of Germany, and victor over the Protestant army at the decisive battle of Smalkald—*a monarch who resigned his crowns, and spent his last days in a monastery.*

The letter is dated December 13, 1527, and is written from Burgos, in Spain. The Emperor is answering an appeal, made by Erasmus, against the threatened suppression of his book, by the Spanish clergy. The monarch writes:

"Dear and Honored Sir—Two things make your letter welcome to me. The receipt of any communication *from a person whom I regard with so much affection*, is itself a pleasure, and your news that the Lutheran fever is abating, gratifies me extremely. *The whole Church of Christ is as much your debtor as I am.*"

Observe the date of this warm praise of the "worthless," untruthful Erasmus pictured in *Truth*, in its issue for February, 1916: The mighty Catholic monarch was expressing *affection*, for the penniless scholar whose *Praise of the Folly*, and whose *Colloquies*, had, many years before, acquainted all Europe with the vices, with the crimes, the abuses, and the impostures of *papal* Christianity.

In 1527, Luther's heroic combat with Rome had long been under way; and the Emperor was assuring Erasmus that, not only himself, but the whole Catholic church was under obligations to the peerless scholar.

The letter of Charles continues:

"You have done for it (the Church) what *emperors, popes, princes, and academies HAVE TRIED IN VAIN TO DO. I congratulate you from my heart.*"

A devout Catholic monarch, the most powerful of his time, places the services of his fellow Catholic—humble writer of books—above that of emperors, kings and popes, *because* the work of that marvellous brain and pen had been so effective against Martin Luther!

The letter of the Emperor concludes in these words:

"Take courage therefore. Be assured that I shall never cease *to respect and esteem you.*

Remember me in your prayers."

(The Italics in the quotations from the letter are mine.)

The year before Erasmus passed away, at Basle, (1536) Pope Paul III. presented to him, by the hands of the Cardinal of St. Angelo, a gold cup, so exquisitely engraved that it was said to be worthy of Praxitiles. Following the magnificent gift, came a personal letter from the new Pope to the old scholar; and it was couched in terms of respect and affection, creditable to them both.

I regret that there is not space enough at my disposal now to present the views of Erasmus, in his own language, as to the successive mistakes by which Pope Leo X. and the influences at Rome, had provoked the revolt in Germany. In brief, he blamed the scandalous traffic in "Indulgences" and the still more scandalous manner of it: he blamed those who were responsible for the harsh measures directed at Luther: he paid the highest tribute to the private character and the honest motives of the Wittenberg ex-monk; and, more than all, he lamented the failure of the Popes to make any movement toward *a voluntary reformation*, which would have kept the Roman church undivided.

Erasmus did not possess the bulldog pluck of Luther, nor his stalwart manliness, nor his qualities as a fighter and organizer. In mind and body, he was of a more sensitive, feminine type than the heroic Reformer. But he was ready to attack the doctrines and the methods of Luther, and he did so, more effectively than any other living Catholic was able to do.

The Emperor Charles V. had faced the Reformer at the Diet of Worms; and, being a brave man himself, he doubtless respected the "little monk," who so valiantly braved Emperor and Pope on that historic stage.

Years afterwards, the monarch was in the town where Luther had lived, worked and suffered; and he was taken to see the Reformer's tomb.

The priests and monks who were with the Emperor, urged him to have the grave opened, in order that Luther's bones might be thrown to the dogs, as Wycliffe's ashes had been cast into the river; but the royal Charles answered, royally:

"*I make no war upon the dead!*"

It was left to the petty, contemptible *American* fanatics of today, to not only defile the tomb of Martin Luther, but also that of his greatest Catholic adversary.

You must not suppose that the immunity from persecution enjoyed by the most popular and illustrious European man of letters, was extended to humbler Catholics.

Oh, no! Rome was still offering to its Moloch the sacrifice of burning human bodies. Not the slightest liberty of conscience was permitted to the average priest, or to any layman. Inebriated with heretic blood, the drunken Fury on the Tiber constantly clamored for more, *more, MORE!*

It was this unquenchable thirst for blood, this insatiable craving for absolute power, that was to plunge Germany into the Thirty Years' War, devastate more than a thousand cities, kill off half the population, transform Christians into Cannibals, and set back the empire so far toward the Dark Ages that a Jesuit-taught Hapsburgh emperor would take frenzied delight in the slaughter of his own subjects, saying—

"*Better a desert, than citizens who are not Catholics.*"

In 1528, Erasmus, in a letter to an English bishop, mentions two poor Catholics in France who had been condemned to be burnt "*because they had eaten meat in Lent.*"

Again, Erasmus writes—"Cardinal Matteo said at a public dinner before a large audience, *naming place and persons*, that the Dominicans had

buried a young man alive *whose father demanded his son's release.*"

(Cardinal Matteo was an intimate personal acquaintance of Erasmus.)

It is well known that Sir Thomas More was put to death by Henry VIII., because of his refusal to take the oath that the English monarch was the supreme authority in his kingdom. Therefore, it cannot be doubted that Sir Thomas was a papist of the strictest standard. Being in the Netherlands on a diplomatic mission, after Erasmus had so much enraged the monks, Sir Thomas wrote to his friend, warning him that his life was in danger:

"They mean," wrote More, "to have your writings examined, *with the worst intentions toward you.* Be cautious. * * * You will ask who the parties are. *I fear to tell you, lest you be frightened* by such antagonists.

You see your danger.

The resolution was taken at a supper party, *where they drunk more wine than was good for them.*"

Think for a moment of the significance of this letter, from the most eminent Catholic of England to the most eminent Catholic on the Continent! Sir Thomas More warns his friend Erasmus that certain Catholic prelates, so powerful that More *fears* to name them, have resolved to destroy Erasmus, by selecting heretical passages from his books—which, of course, meant *a secret trial before the Inquisition, where the accusers would act as judges*, and condemn Erasmus to death!

"They have divided your works among them," wrote More; "each is to take a part. The object is to expose your mistakes."

By "mistakes," Sir Thomas meant those variations from orthodox Roman Catholicism which were capitally punished by the Inquisition at Rome and throughout Europe.

Some months after More's warning, which Erasmus had at first been disposed to treat lightly, the storm had reached such threatening violence, that Erasmus wrote—

"You will hardly believe how near I

escaped *being burnt,* the divines at Louvain were in such rage at me. They petitioned the King and the Pope to cease to protect me.

If I do not get a final decision in my favor, there is an end to Erasmus, and nothing will remain but to write his epitaph."

The aristocratic Medicean pope, Leo X., was too much of a man of "wine, woman and song;" too much of a lover of literature, and the fine arts; too fond of sunny life and too little of a "religious," to even seriously think of signing the death-warrant of Erasmus. He didn't even care two straws about the heresies of Martin Luther; and had the Vatican cardinals left him alone, he would not have made *the papal mistake of elevating the Wittenberg monk to the level of the Roman pontiff.*

In fact, Leo X. read the *Praise of Folly,* and laughed over it. Neither he nor its author could understand the deadly wrath it had aroused among the friars, monks and Catholic prelates. Luther declared that if it had been his intention to describe the Roman theologians as they really were, the *Praise of Folly* would have seemed a mild book beside the other.

It should always be remembered that Erasmus did not make his appeal for reform to atheists, skeptics, or Catholic laymen: he made it to the Popes, in personal letters, read to them by the secretary.

Passionately and persistently, he prayed the Pope to draw the line *between religion and superstition!*

The appeals made no impression: the secret orders had become too strong even for the Popes: nothing could be done to cleanse a vast *cloaca maxima,* whose filth and stench covered Europe.

So true it is, that *no organization,* religious, political, economic, or social, *ever voluntarily reformed itself from within.*

Next to the stupendous debt which modern democracy and progress owe to Martin Luther and John Calvin, comes the debt which modern Catholicism owes to those intrepid fighters.

Had it not been for the terrible shock and *scare* which Rome received from those two men, the modern papacy would not possess even that semblance of virtue which compliments the real thing, by *pretending* to be virtuous.

The Woman of Babylon.

Joseph Hocking.

CHAPTER VIII.

THE LAWYER AND THE PRIEST.

It may be thought that such a far-seeing man as Ritzoom would not have sent his name to Raymond, remembering the mission upon which he was engaged. But Ritzoom knew that he risked scarcely anything by so doing. While well known to members of his Order and to those with whom he came into personal contact, he was practically unknown to the great world. He spoke at no big gatherings, his name did not appear on important councils, neither did he do anything to make his name known to the community. He worked in the dark. His hands touched secret springs, he guided public affairs while he himself remained unknown.

As a matter of fact, Walter Raymond had never heard the name in his life, and when he glanced at the card he had no suspicion as to whom he was. The name appeared to him to have a foreign sound, and that was all.

"Will you be seated?"

Raymond's office was neither large nor luxurious. Up to a year ago he had shared two inexpensive rooms with several other men, not being able to afford an office of his own, and now, although he managed to pay for the room in which he sat, as well as a little box behind, where a boy, dignified by the name of "clerk," copied letters and ran errands, there was no evidence of anything like affluence.

Ritzoom noted this at a glance, and drew his conclusions accordingly. Whatever the results of the great trial on which he had been so long busily engaged might be, he was at present only a poor, struggling lawyer, eager for any work that might fall in his way.

"Are you very busy, Mr. Raymond?"

Raymond looked at his visitor before he replied. As I have said, he was not a brilliant man, but he had a large fund of common sense, and he was not one who could be easily carried away by the impulse of a moment.

"A lawyer is always busy," he replied; "but seldom too busy to see clients."

Ritzoom laughed quietly. The answer seemed to please him.

"Then you can give me a few minutes of your time?"

"If I can be of any service to you, I shall be very glad."

For a moment Ritzoom scarcely knew how to begin. This quiet, honest-looking man baffled him somewhat. In early years he had failed to attain his purpose by under-estimating the strength of the man he had to deal with, and he had grown wiser by experience.

"The business about which I have come to consult you," he said, "is rather delicate. It is not quite in the way of conveyancing, neither does it run in the line of litigation."

Here he stopped and looked at Walter Raymond steadily, but the lawyer made no sign whatever. He waited in stony silence for Ritzoom to proceed. This was undoubtedly, from a professional point of view, bad policy, as every lawyer is supposed to try and impress a client with his own special interest in that client's welfare. But Walter Raymond was not a man after that order: he assumed nothing which he did not feel, and he was not altogether at ease in his visitor's presence.

"In short," went on Ritzoom, "I want a lawyer whose name is free from all shadow of taint, who is the soul of integrity, and who can be in sympathy with the aims and objects of my visit. With regard to the first two qualifications my visit here is a sufficient guarantee that you are just the man I need."

Raymond bowed his head slightly.

"The question is," went on Ritzoom, "are you disposed to take the matter in hand?"

"When I know the nature of the business, I will tell you," replied Raymond quietly.

"It is of such a nature that I could not give details until I have some assurance that you will take the matter up."

Walter Raymond hesitated a second, and was about to reply, when Ritzoom continued:

"Of course, the qualifications I have mentioned—a stainless career and strict integrity—are a sufficient guarantee that the business is of the most honourable nature. At the same time, there are certain things about which one must be absolutely discreet."

Again Raymond looked at Ritzoom, and noted the strong face and unfathomable eyes. He felt that his visitor was no ordinary man, and that he had come on no ordinary commission. Moreover, he was far from comfortable in his presence. Instinctively he felt that the man before him was secret, mysterious, and out of the ordinary run of men: as such he disliked him. On the other hand, he was sure that he had not come to him about some trivial matter, and he was eager, for his children's sake, to obtain lucrative business.

"I need scarcely remind you," he said, "that no solicitor would obtain a reputation for integrity without being very careful about the cases he meddles in. Again, I am sure you are well aware that he would be driven out of the profession if he did not regard all confidences as sacred. I have refused many cases in my life, but no would-be client has had to complain that I have betrayed his confidence."

He spoke very quietly, but Ritzoom felt that here was a man who was not easily moved.

"I know I am making a strange request," said Ritzoom; "I know that every solicitor should have the general outlines of a case before he decides whether he will take it up. On the other hand, I am in no ordinary position. I give you my word of honor that no lawyer's reputation could possibly suffer by being engaged in that about which I have come to consult you; at the same time, I could not make it known to you without the assurance that you will devote your best energies to it."

Walter Raymond rose from his chair.

"I am sure I need not detain you any longer," he said quietly.

Ritzoom, however, did not move from his chair, and Raymond's attitude made him unbend somewhat.

"Your conduct makes my desire to secure your services stronger," he said with some degree of warmth. "It is not often one meets a man so scrupulously particular."

"I think you are mistaken," said Raymond, still remaining on his feet. "No lawyer would take blindfoldedly a case which may be utterly hopeless or utterly beyond him."

"It is neither hopeless nor beyond you," said Ritzoom. "It is simply a matter which requires special treatment. As a consequence, it is of great importance, it is of a very remunerative nature, and if successfully carried through it would lead to other things of a very desirable character. Indeed, it is almost in the nature of an appointment."

"In that case," said Raymond, "there is still less need to detain you."

Still Ritzoom did not move from his chair. While not looking the lawyer straight in the face, he was studying him closely. He seemed to be reckoning up the man before him, and to be weighing him in the balances.

"I will go as far as I can," he said presently. "I said at the beginning that I required three qualifications in a lawyer, independent of professional ability."

"Yes," said Raymond quietly, "you insisted on sympathy with the matter in hand without stating its nature."

"True," said Ritzoom blandly. "The fact is, Mr. Raymond, I am a bit of a bungler. Having but little experience with men of the legal profession, and having been led to believe that this same profession is full of subtleties of which I have no knowledge, and with which I have no sympathy, I have doubtless acted foolishly. To be perfectly frank, then, I want a lawyer who is in sympathy with religious objects—one who would work, not simply for his fees, but for the cause he is engaged in."

Raymond sat down. "What are the religious objects?" he asked. "Personally, I am aware of no religious objects which require a solicitor to promise to engage himself on their behalf without knowing their nature."

Ritzoom was silent again; then he went on like a man speaking excitedly.

"No doubt you are perfectly right. You are, of course, in sympathy with religious objects?"

"I trust I have sympathy with all objects which tend to benefit mankind," said Raymond guardedly.

"Thank you," said Ritzoom, rising, "I will think over what you say and probably call again. Good-morning."

Walter Raymond opened the office door and bowed his visitor out.

"What is the meaning of this?" he asked. "That was no ordinary man, and if I mistake not he was here on no ordinary business. However, I have doubtless got rid of him for ever. He will find another man who will engage in his mysterious work."

He toyed with the card that was left.

"Anthony Ritzoom," he said. There was nothing more. No address, no indication of profession or station. The name was engraved on an ordinary piece of cardboard and suggested nothing out of the common.

As for Ritzoom, he walked away evidently in deep thought. Presently he found himself in Temple Gardens, where he sat down. He took no notice of those who sat near, nor of the people who passed to and fro. Men and women walked close to him—some idlers, others busy people on their way to an appointment; some strolled moodily by, others were eagerly talking, but he took no notice. He might have been in the heart of the country, far from the haunts of men, instead of being in the center of the greatest and busiest city in the world.

Presently he lifted his eyes. He could just see the traffic on the river beyond the palings of the garden. The ancient obelisk which stands on the river's bank attracted his gaze.

"Very old, very interesting, but very useless," he muttered; "besides, this climate—this cursed climate——"

He moved impatiently, and was silent for a minute.

"Yes," he went on presently. "This climate destroys everything. Even my faith grows weak when I am in England, while my confidence goes from me. Somehow the typical Englishman baffles me. It is only when they lose their peculiar characteristics that I can manage them. This quiet, dogged strength is disconcerting. An Italian would have swallowed my bait, so would a Spaniard, so perhaps would a German; but I don't know. There is something in the Saxon blood which saps my confidence."

Ritzoom rose and walked towards the Temple station, but before he reached the gates of the gardens he turned back and again seated himself.

"A difficult man, a difficult case," he mused. "Let me sum it up. Old Raymond, a millionaire and a bigoted Protestant. Young Raymond, an impecunious lawyer, who has just begun to get on; a quiet, honest man—a man with no strong religious convictions, but a schismatic at heart; one who would quietly snap his fingers at priestly authority. His wife a weak woman, who yielded to Brandon't first attack, but who, with him to aid her, can make her husband's life miserable; a woman who is feverish to convert everyone to the Catholic faith, and who has set about to convert her children. Because of this there is already a barrier between her and her husband. This man and woman are married according to the English law. but in the eyes of the Church—well, I must leave that to Brandon. Children have had a sham baptism. Eldest daughter in one of our schools. Let me think, now, let me think!"

Ritzoom rose and walked towards the Temple station, but before thought he was asleep. They wondered why a well-dressed man should care to fall asleep in Temple Gardens on a raw, chilly day. But, as may be imagined, he was not asleep. Some men say they can only think at the end of a pen; but Ritzoom was not one of those. By the end of half an hour every detail of the case before him was outlined—everything was clear before his mind; he had made up his mind concerning the course of events.

For Ritzoom shared the belief and feelings of the hero of Alexandre Dumas' great novel: he wanted to be Providence himself, and believed he could be.

"Any fool can sit down and wait for what comes to pass," was one of his favourite sayings; "a wise man shapes things according to his own desires."

Not that he altogether liked his present work: it was somewhat mundane, a trifle sordid. Ritzoom greatly delighted in work which affected the destines of communities. He loved to convert a man of influence and power to his way of thinking, and thereby to silently influence the course of public events. He had often said that had he lived in the time of Henry VIII. there would have been no dissolution of monasteries, and that, had he had the position of Father Parsons, he would never have allowed Philip II. of Spain to be concerned with the miserable fiasco of the Great Armada.

"A wise councillor at the elbow of Elizabeth would have made her willing to marry Philip, fool though he was," Ritzoom maintained, "and then England would have become Catholic again, and not embittered against the greatest Catholic force in the world."

Still, the affair at stake was important. The Church wanted money, and to convert the Raymond family wisely would mean the gathering in of old Raymond's treasures. This did not mean direct influence upon public events, but it did mean the sinews of war. .

He walked towards the new Westminster Cathedral, which was in course of erection. When he reached it he saw a sea of scaffold poles.

"The world has been scoured to raise a few thousand pounds to build this," he reflected, "and we are hampered on every hand for money. Besides, this place will be hidden, even when it is built. We cannot afford to buy enough land. We, the great Church of Christendom!"

He walked away sadly, still thinking deeply.

"A quiet, strong man," he reflected, "but still a kind and honourable one. I must see to it that he succeeds. That will soften his father. A reconciliation will follow. But the old man must learn nothing of the conversion of his wife and children. It requires care—great care."

Three days later, when Walter Raymond returned from his office, his wife passed him a letter.

"I do not read French well," she said, "but I think I've made it out. I don't like the idea a bit."

Walter took the letter and read it carefully. It was signed Gertrude de Villiers, and contained a strongly worded request that Joyce should be allowed to spend the Christmas vacation at the De Villiers' chateau in Normandy.

"I hope you will consent to this," the letter ran. "Your daughter Joyce has become a great friend of my daughter Gertrude, so much so that they have become almost inseparable. I expect this is because they are both Protestants, and are therefore practically alone in a Catholic school. We belong to an old Huguenot family, and thus their influence upon each other is very desirable. There is also a French Reformed Church close to the chateau. Of course, no religious influence is directly brought to bear upon them at the school; nevertheless, the atmosphere is sure to be Catholic, and that is why I am so pleased that Gertrude and Joyce have become such friends. Please say she may come. I enclose a picture of the chateau, which will show you, I hope, that her surroundings will be pleasant. We also keep up the English fashion of observing Christmas, and will promise to take every care of your daughter."

"I don't like it," said Mrs. Raymond when she saw that her husband had finished reading.

"Why?" asked Walter.

"You need scarcely ask why."

"But I do."

"I suppose these French Protestants are very bitter to my religion," said Mrs. Raymond.

"Scarcely," said Walter, "seeing that the De Villers have sent their daughter to a Catholic school."

"That may be; still, you see what this Madame de Villiers says. Besides, I hoped that——"

"Hoped what?" said Walter, when he saw her hesitate.

"I hoped that—that, well, she would be led to the truth."

"That is, I suppose, you intended trying to convert her?" said Walter.

Mrs. Raymond was silent.

"I'll think about it," said Walter. "I do want to see her badly. My heart is aching for her—in fact, just aching for her—but I shall be terribly busy this Christmas. Work is coming in that I did not expect, and this lawsuit presents new difficulties. Even if she comes home, I shall be able to give her very little time."

"Yes, but I shall have her," said Mrs. Raymond. "I shall have her all to myself. She will be able to tell me about the services at the beautiful church connected with the school, and about those lovely processions through the old town of Bruges. And I shall be able to tell her all I've experienced since I became a Catholic. Oh, Walter, if you only knew the joy of faith!"

Walter sighed. "I must think about it," he said, and then he went on with his dinner.

"I'm inlined to agree with you," he continued presently. "No doubt it would be pleasant for Joyce to go to this old chateau, for it is a beautiful place, but I feel as though I must see my little girl."

"She'll want new dresses if she goes there," suggested Mrs. Raymond.

"She'll have to have them anyhow," said Walter. "She will be quite a grown woman now, I suppose. And then there will be the expenses from Bruges here. Still, I feel I must have her home, and I will be with her all I can."

Mrs. Raymond did not seem pleased at the trend of the conversation, but she evidently tried to show no sign of it.

"Yes," continued Walter; "I must write to this Madame de Villiers, telling her of our decision. I'm afraid my French is very rusty, but I dare say I shall be able to manage it."

Mrs. Raymond burst out crying.

"What is the matter?" asked Walter anxiously. "There is nothing wrong, is there? You see we are of the same opinion about Joyce coming home."

"Yes, yes, it's not that; but, oh, Walter, I am miserable."

"Miserable! Why? Are you ill?"

"In body, no. I believe I should be quite well, only——"

"Only what?"

"Oh, Walter, you surely know."

Walter's face hardened.

"I can never be happy until—— Oh, Walter!"

"Has that fellow Brandon been here today?"

"No one has called today."

"Then you've not seen him?"

"I told you no one has called today."

She had been to confession that day, and had had a long conversation with the priest, but she did not mention it.

Walter looked at her steadily, as though he would read her thoughts. The old trust had gone. Still, he did not press his questions further, but took his pipe from the mantelpiece and began to fill it.

"Walter, Walter, I must tell you."

"Tell me what?"

"I cannot go on like this any longer."

"Like what?"

"Living with you as your wife."

Walter was about to say something of an angry nature, but he kept silent.

"I have borne it as long as I can, Walter, and it's so little for you to do!"

"I think you had better go to bed, Lucy," he replied; "you are overwrought."

"No, no. This must be settled, and forever. Unless you will be married according to the rites of the Church, we must be strangers for the future.

"Strangers?"

"Yes, strangers."

"Think, Lucy, what you are saying."

"I have thought, and I have made up my mind."

"Do you mean to say that you will leave me?"

"No; I do not mean that. But I can no longer be your wife."

"Listen, Lucy," said Walter quietly. "Even your religion does not demand re-marriage. I have looked up the matter, and I find that non-Catholic marriages are accepted by your Church."

"I don't care, I don't care. I must obey my conscience. I have thought it all out, and I have come to a decision. For my children's sake I will live in the house; but only as a stranger to you."

Walter looked at her steadily. Her face was flushed with excitement. A look almost amounting to terror was in her eyes; evidently she was much wrought upon.

"Oh, Walter, Walter," she went on, "it is so little I am asking of you, so little. Just to go with me to the church and take me as your wife according to the rites of our faith. No one will know, no one can know. We can go late at night or early in the morning. Won't you do this for me, Walter—for the children's sake?"

The promise was almost upon his lips. As we have said, he troubled very little about the niceties of theology, and he was by no means strict about matters ecclesiastical. Moreover, he was very fond of his wife, and wanted to make her happy. What she had suggested was the line of least resistance, and he longed for the peace and trust of the old days. But there was one thing in what she had said which kept him from yielding to her wishes.

"For the children's sake," she had pleaded.

The words opened up before him an avenue of thought. If he yielded to his wife's wishes, he could no longer refuse to have them baptised into the Roman Church. It meant, moreover, that he had consented to his wife's conversion, and put his seal on that consent by practically participating in her new faith. It would be the first step on a road which, if he entered, would compromise his whole future.

"No one need ever know, Walter; no one. I will never tell anyone. I will take my oath on the crucifix. No one can ever know."

Again she struck a false note. There would be something cowardly about the act. He did not like to do something which he was afraid for the world to know of. The thought was repellent to his truth-loving nature.

"No," he said quietly, "I shall not do it."

Mrs. Raymond threw herself into a chair, and began to sob bitterly, but Walter's heart had become hardened. He felt more than ever that the priest had ruined his home life.

He took some papers from a drawer, and began to write. Evidently the letter cost him much labor, for he wrote slowly and it took him a long time. Mrs. Raymond remained in the armchair, but he paid her no attention.

Presently he finished. The letter was written in French. When he was addressing the envelope Mrs. Raymond looked up. Her curiosity had overcome her grief.

"Who are you writing to?"

"As we are to be strangers in future, it can scarcely interest you."

"Who are you writing to?" she repeated.

"To Madame de Villers."

"Have you declined her invitation for Joyce?"

"No. I have accepted."

He stamped the letter, and went out to post it. When he was gone Mrs. Raymond rose to her feet. "At least Father Brandon will be pleased that I have succeeded in this," she said to herself.

CHAPTER IX.

The Shadow of the Priest.

One afternoon, several weeks after the events recorded in the last chapter, Walter Raymond returned early from his office. He had been working very hard, and, as there was nothing which called for his immediate attention, he determined to go home and spend an hour or two with the children. He felt his estrangement from his wife keenly. She assumed a martyr-like attitude whenever she was in his presence. She cried often; and when she spoke it was in aggrieved and wounded tones. When she went to bed at night she said "Good-night, Mr. Raymond," and then he saw her no more until the following morning. Sometimes she did not get down until he had gone to business, and when he returned home at night it was only to be met with a chilly reception.

For the first few days he took but little notice of this.

"She will soon get over it," he said. "After all, Lucy is an affectionate creature, and will soon see this kind of thing is so much nonsense." But presently he grew irritated. While retaining his quiet attitude, he was nevertheless deeply annoyed by her behavior. Not that she changed his opinions in the slightest. The more he reflected over the matter, the more both mind and heart revolted against taking part in what was to him worse than a fiasco. Nevertheless, he was miserable. The old happy home life was now a thing of the past. The priest had cast his shadow everywhere. When he entered his house of a night, the place reminded him of a vault more than anything else. As a consequence, he stayed at the office later than he otherwise would have done.

But it was not only the attitude of his wife which troubled him. Try as he would to think otherwise, he felt that his children had changed towards him. Somehow the old feeling of comradeship had gone. He saw that they did not refer to him as in former days. They never asked him to come and tell them stories. Rather they glanced at him furtively, and then went to their mother with messages which they delivered in a whisper.

He was not an inquisitive man, and he had always insisted on bringing up his children in the belief that he trusted them entirely. Whenever he asked them a question, he never doubted their answers. Moreover, he never sought to pry into their secrets. "They will be sure to tell me everything if I trust them," he said; and up to a few weeks before his trust had been justified. But lately he had seen a change. They seemed to regard him as a pariah—he was the ghoul at the feast. Even Walter, the joy of his life, seemed to look at him suspiciously, as though he were a creature to be feared.

To Walter Raymond this was bitterness itself. A fond father, he had been ready to sacrifice anything for his children, and now to feel that they were becoming estranged from him was terrible. He persistently drove away the thought that his wife was responsible for this. "It cannot be as bad as that," he said to himself again and again; "it is because I have given them so little time. Business has been so exacting that I have scarcely seen them. I must be more with them, and then the happy old times will come back again."

That was why he hurried home on the afternoon in question. "I shall be in time to meet them as they come in from school," he reflected, "and we'll have tea together, and then I'll romp with them."

His heart warmed at the thought of meeting them. He was not tired as usual, and he looked forward with pleasure to having a long evening at home.

He pened the door with his latch-key, and then went straight into the little dining-room, where his wife sat busily writing. This was an unusual occupation with her, as she had never shown the least disposition in this direction.

She looked up at his entrance, and seemed to be somewhat confused.

"You seem surprised to see me, Lucy."

"Naturally," she replied.

He bent his head to kiss her, but she moved away.

"No, thank you," she said, "I do not wish to be kissed."

Walter sighed as he went out into the passage and took off his coat. "A warm welcome," he said to himself bitterly; "but never mind, the children will be here presently."

He went to his bedroom and changed his clothes. He wanted the evening to be free from even a suggestion of business worry or work of any sort. Just before he returned to the dining room he heard his boy Walter's voice. The boy spoke loudly and cheerily, as was wont, but something seemed to have happened, for he became suddenly silent. When he entered the room he saw the boy give his mother a letter, which she with evident confusion hid from his sight; he saw also that his wife was whispering to him.

Walter gave his boy a kiss, which the lad returned shyly, looking at his mother all the time. A cold fear came into the father's heart; still, he tried to drive away unsettling thoughts.

"Don't hide the letter from me, Lucy," he said. "Who is your correspondent?"

"I do not see that it is any concern of yours."

"You refuse to let me know, then?"

"Certainly. Walter, leave the room."

"No," said the father, "stay, my lad. I want to speak to you."

The boy looked at his father, then at his mother. He walked straight to the door.

"Walter, stay."

The boy hesitated. The tone of his father's voice was peremptory, but he looked at his mother again, and turned the handle of the door.

Walter Raymond caught his son by the arm. "No," he said quietly, "I do not wish you to leave."

He sat down again, and drew the boy between his knees; then he turned to his wife.

"Lucy," he said, "I am sorry things are taking this course, but surely I am entitled to some kind of explanation."

"I shall give you none."

"Who is that letter from?"

"I shall not tell you."

It was not often that Walter Raymond lost control of himself; at that moment, however, he felt that a crisis had come in his life. Still, he kept himself in check.

"Lucy," he said, "I am very sorry you have adopted this attitude. Do you think it is right?"

She was perfectly silent, but she looked threateningly towards her boy, who was pinioned between his father's knees.

"During the whole of our married life I have kept nothing from you," he went on; "even in my business matters I have consulted you."

"Have you told me your clients' secrets?" she asked.

"I have told you everything which has concerned myself," he replied; "I have given you my fullest confidence. Up to a few months ago you returned that confidence. Why am I shut out from that confidence now?"

"You know why: our relations are changed."

Still he kept himself under control.

"I do not like talking about such things before our boy, but you have compelled me," he said; "besides, I do not wish the woman who bears my name to carry on a clandestine correspondence."

Again Walter saw a threatening look pass from mother to child.

"You refuse to tell me anything about that letter?"

"Certainly. You have no right to it. As you know, I do not regard you as having any right to ask."

"Walter," said the father, turning to his boy, "you brought that letter to your mother. From whom did you get it?"

The boy looked at his mother and was silent.

Walter repeated his question quietly, holding the boy's face towards him and looking into his eyes. "You know your old dad trusts you, Walter, and that he has always trusted you. Tell me—from whom did you get that letter?"

"Father Brandon," said the boy.

He opened his mouth to ask other questions, but refrained. He felt sorry now that he had taken this step, sorry that the boy had been brought into the matter. He kissed the lad tenderly. "I'll come up and have a romp with you presently," he said; "and if you like I'll give you your bath and put you to bed tonight. You can run away now."

Young Walter ran away, evidently glad to get out of the room, while Walter turned to his wife.

"Now that you've frightened your child into disobeying his mother, I suppose you are satisfied," she said.

"Oh, I see," he replied. "You had commanded him not to tell me."

She saw her mistake. In her anger she had revealed more than she had intended.

"It would be interesting to know the nature of your correspondence with Father Brandon," he went on.

"I daresay; but I shall not tell you."

"Then you have secrets between you which you will not tell your husband."

"I do not regard you as my husband: you know that."

"But I am your husband. In the eyes of the law I am your husband—aye, even in the eyes of your Church——"

"You know nothing about my Church," she interrupted.

"Anyhow, you tell this priest what you will not tell me?"

"Certainly. As I told you, I do not regard you as my husband."

"You outstep your creed, Lucy; you go beyond even what your Church——"

"What can you know of a Catholic conscience?" she again interrupted.

"Certainly, it seems a curious commodity," replied Walter gravely. "You set our children against their father, and you tell another man what you will not tell me."

"Certainly. You know why."

"And if I were to do what you wish, what then? Do you think it would be right to tell a priest what you would not tell your husband?"

"Of course I would," she replied.

He was about to ask another question, when Rachel and Madaline returned from school. At the sound of their voices he rose to meet them. After all, there is always something in the sound of young voices which dispels angry thoughts.

But again he was disappointed. Try as he might to dispel the thought, he could not help feeling that all was changed between them. A subtle influence had been at work which had raised an invisible barrier. The children no longer rejoiced in his presence. They seemed to regard him with a kind of fear as one with whom they could not speak freely. He did his best to break this down, but failed. Still, he stayed with them. He had come home to spend the evening with his children, and he determined to do it, and gradnally he felt that in spite of everything the barrier was being removed.

This feeling, however, was presently dispelled.

"I'll hear you say your prayers tonight," he said. "Of late I've not got home soon enough to hear you, but tonight I will."

Immediately there was a chilling silence.

"Don't you want me to?" he said, kissing Madaline.

"No."

"Why?"

"I'd rather not, please."

"Rather not have dad with you when you say your prayers?"

"It isn't that, dad."

"Someone told you not to. Is that it?"

The child nodded.

"Did Father Brandon tell you?"

"Yes, dad."

Walter did not wait longer. The atmosphere of the home seemed poisoned. His children had been taught to distrust him, avoid him. Another had taken his place to exercise authority over those who had hitherto loved to do his will.

I will not repeat the words which Walter Raymond uttered as he left the house.

Never until now did he realize the change which had come over his home. That his wife had been alienated from him he felt bitterly, but he still rejoiced that his children loved him and trusted him. Their young hearts were free from the canker that had entered his wife's heart. Now, however, he felt that they had been slowly poisoned against him. During the hours when, early and late, he had been away from home the work had been going on. Slowly, little by little, and almost imperceptibly, they had been taught to despise him.

"It is all owing to that advertisement," he said between his teeth, as he walked towards Chelsea Bridge. "It is all because I wanted a cheap school for Joyce."

This led him to consider how he stood.

"After March I shall have money," he reflected, "but at present I am simply tied hand and foot."

The case to which we have referred had not yet been settled, but he felt sure that when it was settled it would be in favor of the side for which he had been engaged. Still, this did not bring him ready money, and he was not one who would mortgage his future in any way. Up to the end of March, therefore, he would have to be careful of every penny.

"Yes," he said, "after March I will make an end of this I'll send all the children away to good schools—good, healthy, Protestant schools—where they shall be free from the——"

But he did not finish the stntence. He saw the difficulties which arose. Even after March he could not afford to send all four children to good English schools. They must remain at home, and while they were home they would be under their mother's influence. Still he could manage to do something for Joyce and Madeline. Evidently Joyce was not so much influenced by the teaching of the School in Belgium; otherwise she would not have desired to spend her Christmas with a girl who was a pronounced Protestant and who lived in a Protestant home. For the present, therefore, she would be safe, and so he could leave her at Bruges without fear.

But oh, the tragedy of it all! All the old trustfulness and happiness destroyed in less than a year! It was now the end of January; thus only nine months had elapsed since Brandon had first entered his doors.

What should he do? Should he prohibit his entrance to the house, and forbid him to hold converse with his children in any way? But what was the use of that? His wife would set his every wish at defiance, and she would refuse to tell him what had taken place. Or, even if she told him, he was not sure she would tell him the truth. More than once he had been doubtful about the statements she had made; now he saw that she had deliberately deceived him. No doubt she would try and justify her deceit; nevertheless, she had deceived him, and he could never trust her again.

Still, he must think about it. When the great lawsuit was over he would have more time, and he would take wise and necessary steps. After all, he might be unable to undo the evil which had been done.

"Is that you, Walter?"

"Why, it's Ned!"

"I was just on the way to your house, Walter."

"And do you know, Ned, although I had no definite thought of going to your diggings, I am sure I was on the way there."

"Well, and which shall it be now? Shall I go to your house or will you come to my 'digs?'"

"Let us go to your 'digs'—we shall be quiet there."

Harrington turned without a word. He saw that something was the matter with his friend, and, although he asked no question, he longed to know what troubled him.

"Spring will soon be with us," said Harrington, as they passed by Cheyne Row.

"Will it?" said Raymond. "Everything feels very wintry with me."

"Anything gone wrong?"

"Yes, everything."

"Nonsense. The case is ours, my friend; I am perfectly sure we have no need to trouble on that score."

"Oh, no, it's not the case. We are safe there, and work is coming in like one o'clock; but, but—I say, Ned, I want your advice."

"What about?"

"Wait until we get to your diggings, and I'll tell you."

No further word was spoken until both sat by a good fire in Harrington's sitting-room. The young barrister opened a box of cigars, and the two began to smoke. But Raymond was silent: he was not a talkative man, and even to his friend he felt a difficulty in broaching the subject which lay so heavily on his heart.

It's this—this——" he stammered at length; but he did not complete the sentence.

"I quite understand," said Harrington.

"I expect you know what I would say."

"In a degree I daresay I do."

"The worst of it is, the children seem to turn against me. That fellow seems to be getting them more and more under his thumb. I should not be surprised if—if he isn't scheming to get them baptised into his Church—and all the rest of it."

"Didn't you know?" said Harrington.

"What?"

"Your children have been baptised."

"When they were babies, yes."

"No, not that. Three days ago they were baptised into the Roman Church."

"What!"

"It is as I say."

"You are sure?"

"A man who knows Brandon well told me only this afternoon. That was one of the reasons why I was on my way to see you to-night."

Walter Raymond said nothing. He sat quietly looking into the fire. The news he had just heard explained many things.

"This is very—interesting," he said presently.

"But surely you knew?"

"This is the first I have heard of it."

Again he lapsed into silence, while Ned Harrington, true friend that he was, did not make matters worse by talking.

"Thank God, I have Joyce left," he said presently.

Ned Harrington shook his head.

"Surely you have heard nothing about her?"

"No; only I doubt your words. You must remember that Joyce has been the best part of a year under their influence, and from what you have told me she is an imaginative, sensitive, impressionable girl."

"Yes, yes, she is all that; but she is very intelligent, she can see through a fallacy easily."

"How old is she?"

"She must be about nineteen now—yes, nearly nineteen. Quite a young woman in years."

"She is the only one of your children I have never seen. What is she like?"

"A beautiful girl, Ned. I know I am prejudiced in her favour, but she is a beautiful girl—no man can help seeing that. She never had a chance. You know why. I have been so beastly poor. Then my wife's health was so bad that Joyce had to be housekeeper and servant and nurse altogether. Her education was terribly neglected, and I was unable to pay for her to go to a good school. That was why I sent her to this place in Bruges. It was so cheap, and it sounded all right. It is nearly a year ago since I saw her, and my heart is just hungering for a sight of her."

"Why hasn't she come home for her vacations?"

"Well, the truth is, I was persuaded that to let her come home for the midsummer vacation would unsettle her mind. You see, it was the first time she had left home, and I was led to believe that it would be better for her to stay at school. Besides, even the journey from Bruges and back costs money, and I had the others to think of. Well, when we were nearing Christmas, I got a letter from some French Protestants, whose daughter is at the same school, beseeching me to let Joyce spend the Christmas vacation at their chateau in Normandy. They pleaded that they were Protestants, and, as Joyce had made such friends with their daughter, it would be mutually agreeable to the girls if Joyce could go to their house. I should not have accepted, but, as you know, my wife has become a very ardent Papist, and she told me she was longing to get Joyce home that she might lead her to the true faith. This and other things decided me. I did not want Joyce to come home and see that—well, the truth is, Ned, we have no home-life now."

"So you consented?"

"Yes, I consented."

"What is the name of these people?"

"De Villiers. They belong to an old Huguenot family, and are strong Protestants. They sent me a picture of the chateau, a beautiful place, and I suppose Joyce had a splendid time."

"And yet you are a lawyer, and took a very respectable degree at Cambridge!" said Harrington.

"What are you driving at?"

"Can't you see, my dear fellow? Do you think that strong Protestants, old-fashioned Huguenots, who live in a chateau, would send their daughter to a Catholic school? Can't you see that it was a ruse to keep her away from your influence a little longer?"

"But my wife protested against her going there. She objected to her going to a house where there was such a strong Protestant feeling."

Harrington was silent, but Walter Raymond saw an amused smile playing around his lips.

"I'll see that she comes home this coming Easter, anyhow," said he grimly.

"Yes, I should insist on that," said Harrington; "but—but—"

"But what?"

"Nous verrons," said Harrington.

"Of course you'll come and see us when she comes home, said Raymond.

"Of course," said Harrington.

The next two months brought Walter Raymond very little pleasure; but when April came a new light shone in his eyes, for the time drew near when his eldest daughter Joyce, who was now a woman grown, should come home from school,

CHAPTER X.

JOYCE'S HOME COMING.

A week before Joyce was expected home, Walter Raymond again sat in his friend's room.

"I'm as excited as a boy," he said. "You do not know, you cannot tell how I feel, Ned. I have not seen her for a year. Just think of it—a whole year! We were always such chums, too, Joyce and I. Do you know, I am going to be downright lazy this Easter! At last I can afford it. We have won our case, and, although matters are not all squared yet as far as I am concerned, I am actually comfortably off where money is concerned."

"Serve you right," said Harrington. "I know you've waited long enough and worked hard enough."

"Yes, I have. Of course, I am not in clover yet; but the way is plainer. I've been able to send Joyce enough money to make her believe in a fairy godmother. I should have liked to have seen her face when she read my letter. I told her to go to the best costumier in Bruges and get a real lot of finery. Bless her heart! The thought of her coming has made me feel twenty years younger. People will think us a pair of lovers when they see us walking out together."

"Have you asked her whether she has changed her religious views?" asked Harrington.

"No," replied Raymond. "My Joyce would have told me if she had."

"I say, Raymond, did you ever instruct your children in such matters? Did you ever explain why England became a Protestant nation, and tell them of those things for which our forefathers suffered and died?"

"No," said Raymond, "it has always been my belief that children are like plants. Place them in the sunshine and amidst pure surroundings, and they'll grow all right."

"Yes, but even plants need to be given the right direction in life. Do you think either your wife or children would have been led as they have been if you had done your duty?"

Raymond was silent, but a frown settled upon his brow.

"You never told me what you said to Brandon after you learnt that your children had been baptised into the Roman Communion."

"No," said Raymond quietly. "Besides, there's not much to tell you. When I left you that night I considered all sorts of ways by which I could kick up a row; but as you know, I am one of those fellows who sleep on things. Still, I did go to him."

"Ah!" said Harrington eagerly.

"Yes, I called at his house the next night. I followed him home, so that I might be sure of finding him in."

Raymond was quiet a minute. He seemed to be trying to repress feelings of anger that were arising in his heart.

"It was no use," he said presently.

"Why? Do you mean to say he got the better of you?"

"We had no common ground," said Raymond. "I spoke as a man, an Englishman. I spoke from the standpoint of honor and fair play. He spoke as an ecclesiastic, a Jesuit. I was cold and sar-

castic, but I could not pierce his hide. I asked him whether it was a
part of his code of honor to creep into a man's house and seek to
poison the mind of his family. He replied by saying that he was a
priest who worked for eternity. That by and by I should thank him
for leading my family into the light, but that meanwhile he was
willing to bear persecution for the sake of one whom he called his
Master. Oh, he was urbane, suave, and smiling all the time."

"And you kept your temper?"

"Oh, yes, I managed to do that; but I found it very difficult.
You see, the fellow's hide was as tough as that of a crocodile. He
adopted an air of superior pity: I was in darkness, and that sort of
thing. He said that, like his Master, he was come to set husband
against wife and child against parent, and that he did it for their
eternal salvation. Embittered lives and desolated homes seemed
nothing to him if thereby he could extend his creed. In fact, he almost made me an atheist as I listened."

"And yet people will send their children to Catholic schools—for
cheapness."

"Yes, I was wrong, I know. But I did not know, I did not care.
One religion was as good as another to me, if men were kind and
true and loving. But now I see my mistake. Never mind, Joyce
will be home soon."

"I hope she'll not disappoint you."

"Why so, Ned?"

"I can't forget that this is one of the Romanists' most popular
methods of winning converts. They are establishing schools everywhere, and advertising the fact that they will give a liberal education for the most absurd prices. Their teachers are nuns who work
for nothing, and so they can afford to do what honest, healthy
schools cannot afford. Thus the poor and the unwary are trapped.
We English give a home to all the outcasts of Europe, and in one
way I am proud of our position; nevertheless, we ought to be careful. Monasteries and nunneries are being shut up in Catholic countries because their governors will not abide by the law; so they come
to Protestant England. Here they can do what they like. These
institutions are dumped down in our midst, and they are not subject
to the same conditions which obtain in other similar places. We
have no right to inspect or make inquiries. Children can be born
and people can die in these places, and the outside world be no wiser.
And we purblind English people make but very little stir."

"Oh, you bigoted Protestant!"

"I don't think so. I have simply read the history of my own and
other countries, and I know that wherever the priest gains power,
ruin and desolation follow."

"My Joyce shall leave this place, at all events," said Walter.

"Don't be too sure," said Harrington.

"Why, man, do you mean to say that——"

"I say nothing, Walter. All I know is that when an impressionable, imaginative girl, with no very strong religious convictions.
is placed for a year in a convent school, where all the influences are
in favor of Roman Catholicism, you can be sure of only one result."

"And that?"

"Think for yourself," said Harrington.

"A few days later Walter Raymond went to Dover. He had arranged for Joyce to come by the boat which arrived from Ostend in the middle of the afternoon, and he determined to be there to meet her. He said nothing to anyone of his determination, for he was beginning to realize a vague fear which he could not understand. He felt that somehow underground influences were at work, and that it behooved him to be watchful. It might be that events had simply poisoned his mind; all the same, a vague uneasiness possessed him. His home was no longer the same. His wife maintained her cold distant behavior, his children seemed to regard him with distrust and fear, and all this was owing to the influence of the priest in his home. This made him fear for Joyce, and he wanted to have a talk with her before she met her mother. He had gone to Dover from Holborn Viaduct, and arrived there an hour before the boat was due. He therefore walked towards Dover Castle, and then, when he saw what he believed to be the boat from Ostend appear, he hurried back to the landing-place.

He was passing the Lord Warden Hotel when he stopped suddenly. Standing in the vestibule of the hotel, he saw two men in clerical attire. One was father Brandon; the other, although his appearance seemed strange, reminded him of someone. Scarcely knowing what he was doing he stood and looked at them, and presently their eyes met. Father Brandon gave him a bland smile, but the other turned away his head.

Annoyed as Walter Raymond was to see Brandon, his thoughts turned to the stranger rather than to him. Where had he seen the man before? He could think of no cleric like this man, and yet he felt sure he had seen him before. The large and somewhat fleshy face, the square features, the unfathomable eyes, where had he seen them before?

The stranger's presence made him feel uncomfortable, too. Somehow the thought of meeting Joyce did not give him so much pleasure as before. What was Father Brandon doing at Dover? And who was the dark, strong, mysterious-looking man who spoke with him?

The sound of the boat's whistle, however, caused him to hurry towards the pier, and a few seconds later he forgot the priests in his endeavor to pick out Joyce among the passengers who stood on the deck of the vessel.

Nearer and nearer she swept to land, while Walter Raymond's heart beat loud with expectation and joy. To meet his eldest daughter, after a year's absence may seem a little thing to many people; but to the fond father it was an event of no small importance. His eye passed swiftly from one to another, but he saw no one like Joyce. Could it be that something had kept her away?

"Is this the boat from Ostend?" he asked of a sailor.

"Yes, sir. She's pretty crowded, ain't she, sir? You see, lots of people are coming over for Easter."

"Have they had a good passage, do you think?"

"A bit choppy, sir. You see, there's a stiff breeze against 'em. I expect a good many will be rather seedy."

Presently his heart gave a leap. Yes, that was Joyce, with several other girls. But why were they clustered around those nuns? He supposed that they had accompanied them across.

There was the usual crush up the gangways. Many of the passengers hindered progress by carrying baggage which they found difficult to manage. Others looked pale and ill, as though they had spent a miserable four hours, as undoubtedly they had.

Walter tried to attract Joyce's attention, but in vain. She kept with the other girls, while the nuns evidently watched them with a jealous eye.

As they drew nearer Walter Raymond saw that the year's absence had made a great difference in his daughter's appearance. Whatever else the school had done for her, it had evidently agreed with her health. Moreover, he could scarcely believe that this tall, handsome girl was the child he had nursed, and who had been maid-of-all-work in his home. She was no longer a child—she was a woman. She had put up her hair, and the new clothes she had obtained were those of a young lady, and not those of a school girl.

He could have shouted for joy as he saw her. Yes, the year had changed her wonderfully. She was no longer the shabbily dressed child, who had suffered so many disadvantages because of his poverty, but a healthy, finely-grown, and beautiful young woman. The keen wind had brought the color to her face, and she was apparently full of vitality and energy. Father Brandon was evidently right when he told him that the school was healthy, and that the girls had a happy time.

"Joyce," he cried, as she stepped on to the landing stage. It was evident that she had not expected to see him, for she gave a start of surprise. For a moment Walter was not sure that she was pleased to see him, but only for a moment. A still brighter colour mounted her cheeks, and her eyes flashed with joy.

"Dad!" she cried, and they were locked in each other's arms.

The nuns looked on disapprovingly, but they did not speak. Walter had forgotten all about them—he held his child in his arms.

"I am glad to see you my darling," he cried again and again. "Do you know I could not wait until your train got to London? I felt I must be here. In fact, I once thought of going over to Ostend, but my business would not allow me. But you do look well, my little maid! I hardly knew you at first. And Joyce, those new clothes look nice."

"And I'm so glad to be home, dad."

"You can still talk Enligsh, then?"

"Just simple sentences, dad. But do you know, after hearing and speaking nothing but French and German for a year, English seems a bit funny."

"Does it? Well, you have the Continental air. By the way, Joyce, I've been awfully extravagant, I have taken a first-class ticket for you."

The girl's face fell.

"What's the matter?"

"I have to go in the carriage with the others."

As if to confirm his words, he heard a woman's voice in French saying: "Now then, all this way. Mademoiselle Raymond, we await you, and Father Brandon has some tea for you."

The girl turned to obey, but Walter Raymond would not have it.

"I will take care of my daughter," he said. "I have secured a seat for her."

"I have orders from Father Brandon," said the nun, still speaking in French. "Come, mademoiselle, there is no time to wait. I am sure monsieur does not wish to interfere with the arrangements of the school. When we are arrived in London I will hand over my charge to monsieur."

"Ah, Mr. Raymond, I quite understand your desire to have your daughter with you, but really I think it will be better for the discipline of the school if all the pupils travel together, and I am sure you do not wish to upset our arrangements. Come, my child."

"Thank you, Father Brandon, but I will relieve you of all responsibility; my daughter goes with me. Come, Joyce, my darling."

He saw a look pass between his daughter and the nun, but his mind was so full of thought of having Joyce with him that he scarcely heeded it. Nevertheless, he could not help noticing that the glad look had gone from his daughter's eyes.

"Lucky," said Walter Raymond, as he entered the carriage. "I believe we are going to have the compartment all to ourselves. There's the boy with the tea; that's right. Here you are, Tommy," and in his gladness of heart he gave the boy a liberal tip. "The tea is actually hot," he said to Joyce; "isn't this splendid?"

The train moved away from the pier, and as Walter Raymond thought that he would have his child all to himself until they reached London, he felt that he was the happiest man in England.

"I can't make it out, my little maid," he said.

"Can't make out what, dad?"

"That you are my little maid, Joyce. Why, you are actually a young lady, and you look so well, and, if it will not make you vain, so bonny."

The girl laughed with pleasure. Yes, she was a beautiful girl, and the sight of her father and the pleasure of home-coming made her heart beat high with joy.

"I must really have another kiss."

"Dozens, dad. There, let me sit on your knee, just as I used to in old days."

He caught her to his arms and kissed her as thought he were her lover.

"God bless you, my darling," he said again and again. "It is so good to have you."

"And it's good to be had," she laughed.

"And you've had a happy year, my little maid?"

"Very, dad."

"I can't think of you as a schoolgirl. You are so well grown, so much like a young lady who has left school."

"Yes, I've grown a lot. But even as it was, I felt my age awfully when I went. You see, I was so backward. But I've got over that."

"You have got on well in your studies."

"Sister Theresa says I've done wonderfully, while all the girls say I've put three years' work into one. Anyhow, when you look at my report you'll see that I've simply raced from form to form."

"That's splendid. And your languages?"

"That's where I've done best of all. You know I was always fond of studying French and German when I was at home; and, of course, when I got there I found that nothing else was spoken. I was not allowed to speak English."

"Not even out of school hours?"

"No, not even then. You see, the sisters were ever with us, and they invariably spoke either in French or German."

Walter Raymond was silent a few seconds. He did not like the thought of the nuns always being with his child, still he hoped it was all right.

"Joyce," he said presently, "what did you think when your mother wrote to you and told you she had turned Catholic? Weren't you surprised?"

"Surprised? Oh, no."

"I thought you would be?"

"No, not at all. Why should I be? It was very natural."

Again Walter Raymond was silent.

"Do you know that your brothers and sisters have also been baptised into the Catholic Church?"

"Oh, yes, I knew the day after they were baptised."

"Who told you?"

"Mother wrote and told me. I say, dad, why have I to keep my conversion a secret?"

"Your conversion!"

"Yes, besides, I did not want to be received into the Roman Church, at least not then. I should not have consented had you not expressed your desire that I should be?"

"I expressed my desire, Joyce!"

Walter Raymond spoke in tones scarcely above a whisper; in fact, he could scarcely speak at all.

"Yes, mother wrote months ago, saying that she and the children were Catholics, and it was both her wish and yours that I should also be baptised. Don't you remember? I wrote to you about it, but, as I got no reply, I naturally concluded that you left it all to mother."

Walter Raymond was on the point of telling her that he knew nothing about it, but he reflected that to do so would be to tell his child that her mother was a liar. For a moment he longed to do this, but he was not a man who acted on impulse, and so he was silent.

"And so you are a Catholic now, Joyce?"

"Yes, dad."

"And are you happier since you became one?"

"No, I don't know that I am. Only, of course, I saw how wicked it was to be anything else, and how wrong it was to stay outside the Church."

"Did they seek to convert you, then?"

"No, I don't think so, only everything made me feel how wicked it was not to be. But even although I felt it was wicked, I didn't want to be like the others were, and, as I said, I did not feel like consenting, but, as you know, dad, I wanted to do exactly what you desired.'

"And do you feel that you are bound by the Church now?"

"Oh, yes, dad. How can it be otherwise?"

Walter Raymond's heart grew more and more bitter. It was with difficulty that he refrained from telling Joyce of the change that had come over their home, and of the way he had been deceived; but he was a forbearing man, and kept silent.

"You enjoyed your Christmas, Joyce. Oh, it was hard to let you go with those people!"

"Then why were you so anxious for me to go, dad?"

"I thought you wanted to go with your friend—Gertrude, I think you call her?"

"But I would rather have come home. Besides, two of the sisters went with me, and so it seemed as though I were at school all through the holidays."

"The sisters! Do you mean the nuns?"

"Yes of course."

"But Madame de Villiers told me—that is, I thought that the De Villiers were Huguenots."

"Oh, no, they are very strict Catholics—that is, all except Monsieur de Villiers: he is an atheist and believes in nothing. I believe they were Huguenots at one time—in Cardinal Richelieu's days, I think; but now all the family except Monsieur are very strict in their religion."

Walter Raymond felt as though the ground were dug away from beneath his feet. On every hand he had been deceived; more and more he realized that a new standard of morality had been introduced into his family life.

"But, dad," went on the girl, "why have I been told that I must say nothing about my conversion?"

"Are you to say nothing about it?"

"Yes, and can't understand it. If it's my duty to be a Catholic, and of course it is, for, as it was soon made plain to me, there can be no other true religion. But I do not see why I should keep it a secret. Of course, I can't help talking with you about it; but why do you wish me to say nothing to Walter and Madaline?"

"Were those your orders?"

"Yes. When I went to confession this morning Father Leclerc told me to talk to no one in England about my change of faith, except my mother."

"And you will obey him?"

"Why, dad, of course I must; I cannot do otherwise. Father Leclerc is terrible in his penance—simply terrible, and I dare not think of disobeying him."

"I wonder that you dared to tell me."

"Why he meant you, when he told me to speak about religion only to mother. How could he think of excepting you? Still I cannot understand."

Walter Raymond thought a moment. "I think I see the reason," he said to himself. "The priest *did* mean that she was not to speak to me about it. That is why Brandon and those nuns wanted to have her to themselves from Dover to London. They were afraid of what I should say and do; they did not want me to know how I have been deceived all this time. It is all plain enough. Well, on the whole, I am glad, for I don't want it to be known that Joyce is a Catholic. No, I'll say nothing to anyone about it, not even to Harrington. I should be ashamed to tell him."

Walter Raymond was only partly in the right. The reason why Joyce was commanded to say nothing about her conversion lay far deeper than that he should be kept in ignorance of the way he had been deceived, for Walter Raymond did not know Father Ritzoom had been at work.

(Continued in Next Issue.)

EDITORIAL NOTES AND CLIPPINGS.

WILLIAM MAKEPEACE THACKERAY—creator of Becky Sharp, Colonel Newcomb, Jos. Sedley, Major Pendennis and the Marquis of Steyne—had the greatest admiration for Henry Fielding; and Thackeray, in his Lectures, pays the warmest tribute to his immortal predecessor in the realms of fiction.

As every one knows, the chief work of Henry Fielding, his masterpiece, is *Tom Jones*.

It so happens that Chapter XI. of *Tom Jones* begins as follows:

"As in the season of *rutting* (an uncouth phrase, by which the vulgar denote that gentle dalliance, which, in the well-wooded forest of Hampshire, passes between lovers of the ferine kind) if, while the lofty-crested stag meditates the amorous sport,"—any other animal should interrupt, Sir Stag will become infuriated because of this intrusion upon the privacy of his mate and himself.

Now, in a temporary aberration of intellect, I assumed that what Fielding had done and Thackeray had eulogized, could safely be done by *me;* but the best government the world ever saw was persuaded to take a different view.

I am perspiring, right now, under an indictment which charges me, in one distinct count, with the use of that word "rutting."

Uncle Sam, you know, is in his second childhood, and is becoming very much of a dotard.

Else, how can you explain *his* use of the "uncouth phrase," after his prosecution of *me?*

In November, 1915, he was exerting much energy, pleasing the Pope, to convict me of a *felony!* because of my use of the word "rutting;" yet, in February, 1916, *he used the same word himself*, in his Weekly News Letter, issued from his U. S. Department of Agriculture.

This expensive News Letter is one of the consumers of the 300,000,000 pounds of print-paper used annually by Uncle Sam, who thereby enormously increases the price of that necessary commodity to other publishers.

In the Weekly News Letter for February 16, 1916, there is a most practical and exhaustive article on the subject which is so interesting to all right-thinking people, namely—

"THE DOMESTICATING OF MINKS."

There are ten varieties of this versatile animal—Uncle Sam says—and each one of the ten is capable of Domestication.

Until domesticated, minks prefer a diet consisting of chickens, ducklings, goslings, peacocklings, turkeylings, and guinealings, but when taken in the house, as it were, they soon learn to eat whatever is set before them, as all well-mannered creatures should.

At least, that's what the U. S. Department of Agriculture says.

Never having lived in the same house with a mink, myself, I can neither deny nor affirm what Uncle Sam asserts.

This Weekly News Letter gravely—and no doubt veraciously—states that, when the mink has been taken into the house, as it were, he becomes fond of breakfast-food, oat meal, corn meal, rice, milk, and beef.

The interesting article concludes itself in the following language, which, according to Uncle Sam's indictment of me, is "lewd, lascivious, obscene, and filthy," calculated to deprave public morals, and unfit to be spread upon the minutes of the court:

Breeding and Young.

Usually the rutting season comes in March or April. The animals then may be kept in pairs, or one male may be used for five or six females.

My! my!! Uncle Sam not only uses the word "rutting," but delicately intimates that one gentleman mink "may be used for five or six females!"

Oh the shameless polygamous males, and the scandalous polyandric females!

Uncle Sam says of the male mink, about the same that I said of the young and lusty Roman priests.

Monks and minks: what's true of the one, will fit the other.

Now that Uncle Sam has become my accomplice in the crime of sending indecent stuff through the mails, he should either *nol pros.* that indictment, with profuse apologies, or he should be ready to go to jail with me.

George Miner, writing of Mexico for the McClure Syndicate, says—

The Spanish priests were all banished outright. That order also included a number of Irish priests who had been educated in Spain and sent here, and some Italians. The native priests were allowed to remain, but I can't imagine where they hide themselves.

The priests did not go away empty handed. It has been proved beyond a doubt that they took large sums of money with them, as well as vast treasure in the line of gold and silver plate and works of art.

Most of the exiled clergy went to Cuba. Others went to Spain and France and a few to the United States. I have heard of men asking for alms in the United States who claimed to be exiled Mexican priests who had been driven peniless out of the country. I suspect they were impostors. That they were driven away may have been true enough, but I doubt the peniless part of it.

The Archbishop of Merida, the first prelate in Yucatan to hold so high a title—as it had only been a bishopic before—is the most conspicuous of the clerical exiles from here. He went to Havana. When his trunks were unloaded on the wharf there one broke open and proved to be well loaded with gold coin.

This Archbishop's palace was next to the cathedral here in Merida on the main plaza. It was very large—that is, it covered a great deal of ground, for it occupied almost half of one of these big

blocks. I don't know what it looked like or whether it was a beautiful old structure or not, for Governor Alvaredo has had it torn down and a fine modern building erected on its site which is nearing completion. This will be an art gallery, with the ground floor devoted to the offices of the Commission Regulation del Mercado de Henequen, which is now housed temporarily next to the police headquarters.

The Archbishop also had a county seat in the suburbs which was much like a royal palace. It had originally been a monastery. Many stories were told me of the luxurious life led there by the Archbishop and his ecclesiastical family. This palace was also taken over by the Governor, who has established an agricultural college in it.

"When will you let the churches open again?" I asked the Governor.

"Oh, in a few months," he replied. "As soon as things are well settled and the church has been taught that it must keep out of politics and not try to run the country. We believe in absolute religious freedom. Any creed is welcome here so long as its ministers and members attend to religious matters and leave politics alone. Meanwhile, the people must worship as best they can. I think they can stand it for a little while, although I am sorry to have incommoded anyone in his devotions.

You have been following the correspondence between Professor Woodrow Wilson and the Kaiser's servants at Berlin: you have noted the distinguished consideration which our State Department treats the most ruthlessly unprincipled despot this world has known since the days of Ivan the Terrible, Czar of Russia.

Now read the telegram which our Government sent to its representative in Mexico, and ponder the difference between being a powerful autocrat and being a weak neighbor:

Telegram.

Department of State.

Washington, Dec. 28, 1915, 6 p. m.

American Consul, Saltillo, Mexico:

You are hereby instructed to proceed to San Luis Potosi and bring to the attention of General Carranza the Department's telegram of June 30 last in regard to mining taxes, copy of which you will take with. You will point out strongly to General Carranza that the taxes imposed by the decree of March 1 last and by subsequent modifications thereof are not justified by laws emanating from the Mexican constitution. You will also earnestly state to him that any collection of taxes from mining and smelting interests in Mexico which has been made by reason of the decree and modifications thereof above mentioned is to be regarded only as a deposit, subject to liquidation when more normal conditions have been restored in Mexico.

The Department is informed that some of the American mining enterests, through inability to meet the increased pertenencia tax imposed, have been compelled to suspend payment on certain of their holdings. This, however, is not to be considered as any relinquishment of rights, and you will impress upon General Carranza the importance of his not taking any action that might cloud or endanger the title to such holdings, reserving to the owners thereof the right of redemption at the time stated in the previous paragraph.

Mining and smelting properties in Mexico have endured great hardships during the past few years, paying no dividends during that time and being a drain upon the companies, and the imposition of excessive taxes now, when encouragement should be given, would result disastrously. These mines employ more than 500,000 Mexicans, affording sustenance to five times that number. The resumption of work is desired by the companies, and it is of great economic importance to the de facto government, because every laborer earning an honest wage is a factor in the restoration of peace and order.

LANSING.

Did you know that the law of nations authorized such a dictatorial interference with the domestic concerns of another?

Our Government warns the recognized Carranza government of Mexico that it must not impose taxes on Mexican mines owned by American capitalists!

How about Mr. Hearst's million-acre ranch?

Is it unlawful for the Mexican government to tax Mr. Hearst's Mexican property?

Guggenheim, Rockefeller, Palmer, John Hayes Hammond & Co. have not had a dividend in *so* long that they pant for breath, poor fellows!

Mr. Lansing is deeply moved.

And he bleats that old, old bleat about the thousands of workpeople that these philanthropic millionaires toil for.

The English government has not embarrassed the Mexican patriots in their fearful struggle for independence, nor has the English government preposterously told the Carranza government that it must not levy taxes on the mines, oil-wells, and ranches belonging to Englishmen.

Mexico's worst enemies are the maranding American plutocrats, and the political priests who use the name of God to promote their own selfishly inhuman ambition.

The American Home Weekly says—

It Took Us Twenty-Two Years.

Just at this moment when Americans are most bitterly denouncing Villa and his bandits and while there are many of us that would trample upon Mexican rights and Mexican peoples to "get Villa," it might be well for us to turn back a few pages of our own history and read.

For twenty-two years an American "Villa" harassed, killed, robbed and destroyed in Mexico.

That was Geronimo, the famous fighting chief of the Apache Indians. In the summer of 1862 he crossed the border with eight men, captured a pack mule train and escaped to the United States with his booty.

A year later Geronimo swooped down on a Sonora village, killed one inhabitant and brought back with him to the United States enough provisions to last his tribe a year. Thereafter, whenever the Apaches needed supplies, Geronimo went to Mexico and took them.

Sometimes Mexicans resisted—and were killed and their women and girls taken captives.

In the late '70's Geronimo and his raiders fought a pitched battle with Mexican troops in Sonora and killed them all. No quarter was given.

During all these twenty-two years the Apaches murdered and robbed in Mexico, returning to the United States when closely pressed by Mexican soldiers. Geronimo fought his last battle in Mexico in 1864. He was decisively defeated and never returned.

This is merely one of the reasons why we should "watch our step" while we are in Mexico putting the foot down on Villa, else we trample on rights and dignities of a people who for decades were victims of our own red-skinned "Villa."

It took us sixteen years to suppress Jesse James bandits, and about the same length of time to round up the horse-thieves and slave-stealers led by John A. Murel.

A friend sends me the following, culled from Thackeray's book, "Henry Esmond:"

The noble Prince of Orange burst magnanimously through those feeble meshes of conspiracy in which his Roman Catholic enemies tried to envelop him. After King James' death, the Queen and her people at St. Germain,—priests and women, for the most part—continued their intrigues in behalf of the young Prince James the Third, as he was called in France; and, the young Prince's affairs being in the hands of priests and women, were conducted as priests and women will conduct them—artfully, cruelly, feebly, and to a certain bad issue.

The moral of the Jesuits' story I think as wholesome a one as ever was writ: the artfullest, the wisest, the most toilsome and dextrous plot-builders in the world—there always comes a day when the roused public indignation kicks the flimsy edifice down, and sends its cowardly builders a-flying.

Mr. Swift has finely described that passion for intrigue, that love of secrecy, slander and lying which belongs to weak hangers-on of weak courts * * * the conspiracy succeeds well, until one day Gulliver rouses himself, shakes off the little vermin of an enemy, and walks away unmolested.

Are club women and celibate men in the same boat?

A bachelor of the priest variety is thus reported:

(By United Press.)
Portland, Ore., Feb. 7.—"The worst demon in the lowest depths of hell is no more despicable than the club women who are promoting this latest curse, birth control."

This denunciation, delivered by Father Black from the pulpit of St. Francis' Catholic Church last night aroused the congregation today. The teaching of eugenics in school also came in for a share of Father Black's excoriation.

"There was a time when the printing press was the curse of the world," said Father Black. "Now comes the latest engine of evil in the form of eugenics in our schools."

When 20,000 American priests lock up 58,000 American nuns, more is done for "this latest curse, birth control," than the club women can ever do.

A few weeks ago, one of the Catholic prelates refused to allow the U. S. Flag to enter the church, at the funeral of a Guardsman, thus imitating the example of those Washington Catholics who, during our Civil War, shut their doors against wounded Union soldiers, when the churches of all *Christians* were open hospitals.

When the Romanists had to order a flag for the 4th degree Knights of Columbus, they ordered it from Rome, Italy, where, no doubt, the Pope squirted water or ambier on it, to make it "holy;" but when the Blessed Flag reached the New York Custom House, the frugal Knights balked at paying tariff duties, and claimed free entry for the foreign flag, upon the ground that it was "religious regalia."

But I'd like to know under what head they import lumber from Italy.

In Europe, they have carloads of the "true cross" upon which Christ died, and they have a milk-canful of the Virgin Mary's maternal lacterial fluid.

So far as I know, they haven't imported any of the Virgin's milk yet, but they are fetching pieces of the true cross, with increasing frequency.

Cardinal Gibbons got the first shipment, and Cardinals Farley and O'Connell have imported, since.

Even Emmettsburg, Maryland, has its Relic of the True Cross, and it was "venerated" at a Feast of the Holy Agony a little while back.

Any tariff duty collected on all this Italian lumber?

I don't know. Perhaps it is classed as religious regalia and escapes the Collector.

Be patient: wait for the wagon: Rome wasn't built in a day. As soon as the Pappycrats deem it wise to do so, they'll begin to import parts of the Crown of Thorns. feathers from the wing of the angel, Michael, hairs from the tail of Balaam's ass, and phials filled with the darkness that fell over Egypt.

Who knows? The Pope is so ravenously fond of us, that he may send us one or two of the heads of John the Baptist, and one or two garments which belonged to the Virgin Mary.

As there are sixteen seamless garments, we might be allowed to have one of them, although we had been given to undrstand that the Roman soldiers gambled for this garment and made off with it.

There are forty nails, used in nailing Christ to the Cross, and now possessed by the Catholic churches of Italy: they must be spikes rather than cast nails, and they would fill a small keg.

Couldn't Papa spare us a few of those nails which are 1900 years old, and which miraculously defy the rust?

You will remember that the Empress Helena went to Jerusalem, 300 years after the Crucifixion, and dug down into the ground to find the Cross and the nails.

She found them. It was never any nation's custom to bury a gibbet, or a block, or a cross upon which condemned malefactors had been put to death.

On the contrary, it was the custom to take them down, put them away, and use them again, at the next necessity.

But the Romans, or the Jews, made a new departure on the occasion of the Crucifixion, apparently aware that a Christian church would need the cross and the nails in its business, 300 years later.

With a prophetic desire to oblige—hard to praise too highly—the Jews, or the Romans, dug a hole in the ground, buried the Cross, and the keg of nails, and left word where to find them.

Consequently, when the Emperor Constantine's mother went to Jerusalem to look for the Relics, the task was much less arduous than that of looking for the North Pole.

"Tradition" as to where the wood and the iron had lain in the soil, for 300 years, had faithfully been "handed down," and the Empress was led straight to the spot—by the monks.

I forget just now *who* preserved the Crown of Thorns, and *how*, but I remember that it turned up, as good as new, some 1400 years after the Crucifixion; and Gibbon tells us how the cynical Eastern Emperor sold it to the Western Catholics for a big price, and how it was used as collateral security for large loans of money.

One wicked, irreverent Catholic prince thought more of keeping his ducats than of redeeming the thorns by paying his debt, and he let it go by default.

Then the pius King of France redeemed it, and somehow it got scattered around among all the cathedrals, where the thorns worked many miracles.

In the "Sketches of Venetian History" published by John Murray (Lord Byron's friend and publisher), we find in the second volume, on page 91, the following curious passage:

"In one object of negotiation she (Venice) failed.

The seamless vesture of the Redeemer was still found, or supposed to be found, in the Reliquaries of Constantinople, and the great price of 10,000 ducats was tendered for it by Venice, and refused by the Unbelievers."

These obdurate unbelievers were the Mohammedans, of course, and the date of the event was 1454. It would appear, therefore, that the Unbelievers had great faith in this coat, which was 1464 years old, and whose value they estimated at more than 10,000 ducats.

The truth about the matter may be this: *Mahomet II. was an honest man and refused to sell himself to a disgraceful imposture.*

But as the Romanists of Europe afterwards claimed to own several of those coats, the question arises, Where did they come from, and *when?*

I knew that Jews were experts in the preservation of old clothes, but it is difficult to believe that Gentiles can keep, in good condition, for 1915 years, the handkerchief of St. Veronica, the Virgin's veil, the shoes worn by Christ when a boy, his shirt and girdle, and the towel he used in wiping the disciples' feet at the Supper.

If ever I go to Rome, to kiss the Papa's toe, I mean to insist upon seeing the bone of the finger that the Doubting Thomas thrust into the Savior's side. The Pope has got it, and I want to see it.

I also mean to insist upon seeing those water-pots which held the wine that Christ made at the wedding feast.

This country is getting so dry that we will soon be denied the use of any wine, but no reasonable person could begrudge us a look at the pots.

THE NERVE OF A PRIEST.

Exposure of conditions in Catholic charitable institutions by State investigators so angered the Rev. Father William B. Farrell, the Catholic clergyman who is rector of the Church of Sts. Peter and Paul in Brooklyn, that he issued leaflets and pamphlets calling the investigation an anti-Catholic conspiracy, a public scandal, and a slander factory. Commissioner Strong, who is hearing testimony, supoenaed the the priest to come before him. At first the Rev. Farrell said he should pay no attention to the summons; then he changed his mind and put in an appearance, but vowed he would answer no questions. The commissioner inquired on what grounds he had made his charges against the investigators, and he retorted: "You have a lot of cheek to ask me questions about my private affairs." Evidently, he had been relying on "benefit of the clergy," which denies the right of the State to bring a priest before any civil or criminal tribunal without consent of the bishop. Here is a scrap of the testimony printed in the New York *Times:*

John Kirkland Clark, counsel for Commissioner Strong, read from one of the pamphlets in which Father Farrell had said Commissioner Strong was a former law partner of Mr. McAney.

"I admit that is a mistake," Father Ferrell said. "I have since learned that it was Mr. McAneny's nephew."

Mr. Clark then read from the record in an attempt to get Father Farrell's admission that other statements were not founded on fact, but William S. Butler, the priest's lawyer, announced that he had directed Father Farrell not to answer the questions, because they did not concern the State Board of Charities, but only Father Farrell's private affairs.

"Father Farrell, we are facing each other as citizens of the city," Mr. Strong said. "You published pamphlets in which you stated facts about me and the manner in which I have conducted this investigation. Do you not think it right for us to have a perfectly frank discussion as to these facts?"

"We can have that privately," Father Farrell said.

"But these pamphlets were circulated publicly," said Mr. Clark. "You have circulated false statements."

"I won't let him question my private rights," said Father Farrell. "It is none of your business what I write. The reason that I felt aggrieved about being brought here was that I knew you wanted simply to harass me, to cross-question me, and assassinate me like Tom Mulry."

Extracts were read from Mr. Mulry's testimony in an attempt to show that he had not been harassed. "I understand that Mr. Mulry died of natural causes," Mr. Clark said.

"I am not sure that he died of natural causes," Father Farrell responded. "I have the testimony of his family that he was in perfect health before he appeared here."

Mr. Clark read over the questions relating to instances in which, he pointed out, Father Farrell had made mis-statements of fact from the record, but the priest refused to discuss them.

"I think you have an outrageous cheek to bring me here," he said in answer to one question.

The conduct of the priest illustrates the arrogant attitude of the church. The right of the State to know how the money paid to charitable institutions is spent, the Rev. Farrell denies.—*Truth Seeker.*

Pastor O'Neill Flays Bachelors as Selfish and Useless to World.

Evansburg, Pa., Jan. 20.—In keeping with the leap year season, Rev. H. M. O'Neill, pastor of the Holy Name Church, addressed a gathering of men last night. Father O'Neill painted the bachelor as a man who usually is of little or no value to any community and who with rare exception leads a selfish life and could well be spared.

Bachelors, he said, seldom accomplish much in life. They are not the men who are found at the head of the great governments for the betterment of the community. They are not the leaders in State and civic affairs, but go on in their own selfishness, living out the natural order and rarely doing their share for humanity.

O'Neill is wrong: there is one class of bachelors that do not lead a selfish life, are a great blessing to any community, who accomplish *very* much, who are the powers behind all European and American governments, who take leading parts in controlling literature, theatricals, the mails, the legislation, the courts, and social affairs.

These bachelors do not deserve the severe strictures of O'Neill.

Paulist Father Appointed U. S. A. Chaplain.
Washington, D. C., April 19.—Rev. Edmond J. Griffin, a noted Paulist, prominently identified with the Ancient Order of Hibernians and Knights of Columbus, and recently elected president of the Irish History Club, has been selected for the chaplain corps of the United States Army. He is a native of Ireland, and graduated with the honors of his class in All Hallows' College. He came to this country in 1908. He served in the diocese of Kansas until he entered the Apostolic Mission house at the Catholic University in 1915.

Are the Romanists in politics?

Oh, no; they go after and get the offices, just for the fun of it.

It's not a policy, or a purpose: it's a mere habit.

You can tell that from the following advertisement in *The Sunday Visitor:*

WANTED—Men and women everywhere. Government jobs. $70 month. Short hours. Vacations. Rapid advancement. Steady work. Many appointments during summer and fall. Common education sufficient. Pull unnecessary. Write immediately for list of positions now obtainable. Franklin Institute, Dept. A-203, Rochester, New York.

Here it is, again:

FORMER PHILADELPHIAN APPOINTED NAVY CHAPLAIN.

Service of the Rev. E. A. Duff, of Greenville, S. C., Dates From December 21.

The Rev. E. A. Duff, of St. Mary's Church, Greenville, S. C., and a native of Philadelphia, has been appointed chaplain in the United States Navy. His appointment dates from December 21, but the duty to which he will be assigned has not been designated yet.

Father Duff is well known throughout South Carolina.

Of course, Mr. Duff did not seek the appointment, and no one sought it for

him. It just came upon him naturally, like dew on the leaf.

The *Truth* magazine (papist) publishes the following:

Hymn.to the Blessed Virgin.

At morn, at noon, at twilight dim,
Maria, thou dost hear my hymn.
In joy and woe, in good and ill,
Mother of God be with me still!
When the hours flew brightly by
And not a cloud obscured the sky,
My soul, lest it should truant be
Thy grace did guide to thine and thee.
Now when storms of Fate o'ercast
Darken my present and my past,
Let my future radiant shine,
With sweet hopes of thee and thine!
—Edgar Allan Poe.

If Poe wrote those namby-pamhy, goody-goody lines, they were not thought worthy of a place in his collected "Poems."

Some moongazing Catholic girl, about 18 years old, wrote that doggerel.

If Edgar Poe was a Catholic, the fact did not appear either in his life or his work.

You must have noticed recently how feverishly the papists are playing up every historic name that can be claimed for Romanism.

They were so persistent about LaFayette, whose services to the Colonies were really valuable, that I took the trouble to examine the volumes written by his physician, M. Jules Cloquet, M. D.

The title of the work is, "The Private Life of LaFayette." Nowhere do I find it stated that the gallant and patriotic Frenchman was a Catholic. The chapter on his last sickness and death, I read with particular care, for if LaFayette was a believer in popery, and had time to secure the services of a priest, it is clear that he would have done so.

He was ill several days, and had the amplest time to send for a priest, *but he did not.*

Napoleon had his son, his dynasty, to think of on his death-bed; and he called for a priest, and made the usual motions; but I don't suppose that anyone ever thought that the Emperor would have hesitated to again kidnap the Papa, and lug him from Rome to France, had the Emperor got back into power.

When Napoleon was sick, he was a good Catholic; not otherwise: but La-Fayette did not want any holy grease and humbug mummery around *him*.

"The Household of the LaFayettes" is the title of an exceedingly interesting book, brought out in this country by The Macmillan Company, New York.

It had previously been published in Europe by a London house. The date of the American edition is 1897.

In this work the author, Edith Sichel, quotes the words used by La-Fayette, again and again, *during the last illness of his wife*, and these repeated statements prove that *LaFayette was not only no Catholic, but was an infidel*, without faith in the divinity of Jesus Christ, *and without religious belief of any kind!* (See pages 314, 322.)

Madame LaFayette was a Catholic, but not orthodox, for she was good enough to believe that all good people will escape eternal torture, no matter what their creed. It is her husband who says that *her* Catholicism was really *Catholic*. (See page 313.) With a touching simplicity, this noble Frenchwoman said, of the good people of other creeds, the world over—"I don't know what will happen at the moment of their deaths, but God will illumine them, and save them."

Divine spirit! We wouldn't want a better heaven than earth would be, if it were filled by men and women of such celestial mold.

The author of the book says—"She was always preoccupied about his heterodoxy."

LaFayette himself wrote—"Yet I never saw her mistaken about me (when she was mentally wandering) excepting once or twice for a moment, *when she imagined I was a fervent Christian.*"

Devoted as he was to his heroic and loveable wife, LaFayette was too honest to soothe her last moments by pretending a faith he had never held.

At the last, it was suggested that on her death-bed—"You admire Jesus Christ; *one day you will recognize his divinity.*"

Her husband answered with an affectionate allusion to another subject.

At the last it was suggested that LaFayette leave the room, *as was his custom*, when his wife was at her devotions; but she insisted upon his presence, dispensing with the devotions. (The church's last rites had been administered to her already.) A crucifix was placed upon the bed, in order that she might hold it in her hands while dying. *Instead* she took her husband's hand within hers, and so died.

As to LaFayette himself, he never changed: to the last, he was a deist, like Jefferson, Franklin, Washington, Thomas Paine, Mirabeau, Frederick the Great, Goethe, and Shakespeare.

In Romanist fable, a mythical Maryland priest miraculously crossed the broad Potomac—on a dark and stormy night, when the moon was shining bright—and *smuggled himself*, with his ghostly outfit of pyxes, oils, wafers, crucifixes, candles, and other priestly delicatessen, *into Mt. Vernon*, to give to George Washington the last rites of the Roman church!

Side by side with the Washington fable, the LaFayette legend wants to grow.

Well, let them grow. A couple of lies, more or less, can't help or hurt such a monstrous anachronism as the Papacy—built on forgeries, frauds, falsehoods, and crimes.

Built that way, it can live in no other way, and therefore the logical necessity for more forgeries, more frauds, more fasehoods, and more crimes.

Bourke Cockran, Joe Scott, Pete Collins, Dave Goldstein, and P. H. Callahan are making urgent appeals for peace and concord among all the religious.

To that campaign of chloroform and soothing syrup, the *Truth* magazine makes a timely contribution, just as the Pope did recently, when he savagey denounced Protestant churches as "emissaries of Satan, robbers, pestilential," and so forth.

Says *Truth:*

Nothing is too dark, too hideous or too infamous for the enemies of Catholicy! One of our readers in Portsmouth, Va., has written us and forwarded a clipping from a Norfolk, Va., paper, regarding the tactics of the wolves in sheep's clothing—commonly known as "returned missionaries." If we are to believe those vile detractors, just returned, we would get the impression that the natives of the Southern Republics have scarcely sense enough to come in out of the rain, to eat, sleep or think! Yet in spite of all this the slime-vending missionaries are forced to admit that those same natives have sense enough to see the sham and the fraud of a divided Protestantism. One faith, one baptism, one doctrine, one Jesus Christ, one God—these glorious truths appeal to the natives who seem to enjoy themselves at the cost of the Baptists, the Presbyterians, the the Methodists and the other men-made brands of religion with their divisions, their contradictions and their lies. That's the reason why the mud-slinging missionaries have concocted the well-planned but shameless scheme to which we referred above. The Protestant churches, divided and contradictory, stand as a huge joke in presence of the divinely built, heaven-united Church of all ages and all peoples. That's the reason why the hypocritical preachers have asked for a division of territory for the different Protestant churches. In other words, the lie-preaching hypocrites want to hide the hideous facts from the Catholic natives. Yes, hide the fact that you are divided among yourselves, and therefore not the true church—the end justifies those Protestant deceivers. Yes, hide the ugly fact that you sectarians teach contradictory doctrines, and therefore are not of God, for truth cannot contradict itself. Yes, lie in act so that you may succeed in stealing the divine Catholic faith from the natives. Yes, lie—lie like the devil—so that you may succeed in imposing you shattered Bible upon the natives and teach them divorce, free-love and race-suicide that are fast killing Protestantism in the United States. We call upon the Catholic press of America to herald forth this latest piece of Protestant infamy so that the world may realize what a horrible farce is being enacted in our Southern Republics.

That's fine! Bourke Cockran and Joe Scott and Pete Collins ought to read it to their Protestant audiences,

every time the sap-head Protestants attend one of these well-calculated, deceptive oratorical displays.

Lord! here comes "Father" Peter Scotti, again!

Read what he's done, this time:

Woman Adopts Priest.

It became known in New Orleans last week that Mrs. Louise C. Thomas, 73 years old, and reputed one of the South's wealthiest women, had adopted as her son and heir Father Peter Scotti, formerly chancellor of the diocese of New Orleans. Mrs. Thomas is the widow of Stanley O. Thomas, the cotton king, who left an estate of several million dollars.

Scotti was Secretary to Archbishop Blenk, wasn't he?

And didn't an importunate woman accuse him of swindling her out of $62,000?

And, what's worse, didn't she prove it on Peter, in court?

As I remember the case, there was another holy man acting with Peter in this lamentable business, and this other holy man vanished away.

But you can't tell the women anything against these holy men: they won't believe it.

Rev. Pete Scotti is a middle-aged man, and he must be an orphan, because he has now become the son of a good old dupe who is 73 years old, and who is worth *millions.*

You have to rise early in the morning, if you get ahead of these priests. Generally, they wait until the dupe is about to die, and then they dictate the will; but in the case of old Mrs. Thomas, this Pete Scotti person wasn't taking any chances.

He legally hitched the ancient lady to a post, in her life-time, and now she has got to stay put. Pete is her son and heir; and if she were any kin of mine, I'd caution her about what she eats and drinks. Sons and heirs sometimes grow impatient.

"The Spectator," July 3, has the following in connection with the condemnation and burning of John Huss at the Council of Canstance:

"The deposition of a Pope, John XXII.,

was not the only memorable event in this extraordinary Council. At Constance there begins the story of the rise of Prussia. The house is still standing in which on April 30, 1415, Frederick, Burggraf of Nuremberg, was invested by the Emperor Sigismund with the Mark of Brandenburg. **For four hundred thousand gulden Sigismund had sold the vacant fief to the thrifty Hohenzollerns.** Strange how altered would have been the future of Europe but for this mercantile transaction! Frederick the Great would have been the Count of a petty fief, and Germany and Europe—but it is useless to speculate."

Four hundred thousand gulden!

One hundred and sixty thousand dollars, in our money.

The fief of Brandenburg was vacant, and a merchant of Nuremberg bought it, as he would a house, or a cargo.

With the fief, went the title, Margrave, or Marquis.

The Hohenzollern egomaniac who now claims to rule, by "divine right," one of the greatest peoples on earth has no more "divinity" in his title and position than President Wilson has in his. The Hohenzollerns purchased the titles of Marquis and King, and were *elected* to the position of Emperor. The latter process of getting up higher, is far more creditable than the former; but if elections are divine things, then its bad for divine right. There's our present Congress, for instance—but, as the preachers say, why dwell?

Do you wear a "charm" of any sort? If not, you are doing yourself a rank injustice. You ought to buy a charm. They are cheap enough. But you must be careful as to whom you buy from, else you might be distressed by seeing the vendor sent to jail.

For instance, there was a man—an accused heretic—who was vending Luck Stones. and he is now in jail doing penance for his sins. The fact that he was a common cheat and swindler could not be gainsayed, because Reason tells us that Luck does not dwell in stones, even if there *is* such a thing as luck. So the Law rose in its majesty, and laid that man out.

Then, again, there was a Christian Science healer—named Willis Vernon

Cole—who claims to have cured an afflicted person by prayer; and after the prayer had been followed by the cure, Willis Vernon collected a little *per diem* out of the cured.

Whereupon the Law again rose in its might, and laid Willis Vernon low, in spite of the arguments of so able a lawyer as Samuel Untermeyer.

A fine of $100 was put upon Cole for his lawless behavior. Virtually the New York Appellate Court held that if Cole had cured the sick person with a pill, it would have been an orderly proceeding, but to cure her with prayer and accept pay for it, was a violation of the statutes.

Yet, I have here in my table-drawer a mass of literature in which the Roman Church invites the stupid laity to enter into a *Novena*—a 9 days' debauch of praying—for the cure of all sorts of complaints, for the finding of lost property, for the securing of gainful employments, and for the correction of all sorts of bad habits.

In case of a cure, money is always sent to the priests. In case the lost keys, pocket-book, stolen money, strayed horses. sick cows, etc., are recovered, the dupes send money to the priests. In case the applicant for a good position gets it, money goes to the priest. In case the husband, or the son quits drinking, money goes to the priest—who never quits drinking.

Does the law take notice of *these* cheats and swindlers?

I have at my hand a piece of white cord. not different from any other white cord; but this one is St. Joseph's cord. Saint J., you know, was the eccentric Jew who married a young Jewess. not to beget little Jews, but for the novelty of sleeping with a Jewess who could retain her perpetual virginity.

Saint Joe must have had a perfectly delicious time, enjoying his own and his wife's obstinate purity. No other Jew ever did so; and it was quite right for the Roman Church to make a Saint out of this one who, according to the Bible. does *not* appear to have been a Christian.

It's only in the Roman Church that a Jew can remain a Jew, and yet be a Christian Saint.

These cords of St. J. possess the peculiar merit of protecting you from all diseases, all tragic accidents, all machinations of the Devil; and, if you happen to have lost *your* virginal state, *this cord will restore it to you.*

You can buy the cords in New York, from the priests.

Does the Law come down on *these* cheats and swindlers?

I have here on my table a wretched little pewter medal of the Virgin Mary, warranted to keep your skin whole in the worst of railroad collisions, and to ward off storms, floods, pestilence, fires, and calamities generally.

The priests are selling these "charms" throughout the Romanist world, and their dupes buy them by the million. Does the Law take notice of *this* systematized cheat and swindle?

Does a Fraud order close any mailsack to this disgraceful robbery of the illiterate slaves of a degrading superstition?

Here is part of a letter written me in 1910, by S. Mays Ball, a friend whom I never met, but whose untimely death I deeply deplored:

Dear Mr. Watson: A young friend of mine, now living here, to amuse this doubtless to him, wayward child, brought out to my home a big bunch of Philippine curios, photographs, etc. As the photos., were all so dried-up, in rounds, so to speak, I got little satisfaction from a sight of them.

But he did have at that time, something that was mighty interesting to me and something, I figured would interest you in your Catholic papers, you're writing.

The object was a so-called Charm sold by the Catholic Priests in and around Manilla for $1, or maybe one peso; don't remember which; the wearing of said charm, a book, with funny looking pictures of the Sun, Moon, Stars—All The Old Things—in battle or in ordinary way through life would be a protection for the wearer, guaranteed by the Priests, The Church, etc.

The Charm I saw was taken from a Filipino, killed in battle; the prisoners taken with the dead warrior all had on one of these charms; and, told their captors

that the Church did a land office business in selling these charms.

We laugh at the poor ignorant Filipino who paid a dollar for a "charm" which had as much efficacy as a Luck stone, but the same Roman Church which debauched the mind of the brown man, has at length corrupted that of his white brother.

Consider the almost unbelievable monstrosity of the "St. Rita" medals, sold by Trant's Supply Store, Rochester, New York. The gew-gaw is a wretched little pewter disc, about the size of a five cent nickel. On one face of it, appears the figure of a woman, on her knees, in the attitude of prayer. She is labelled St. Rita. These medals —and also statues of this Italian saint— can be purchased at prices ranging from ten cents to ten dollars.

The booklet which sets forth the merit of Rita; and the miraculous virtue of the medals claims to be published by authority "from approved sources."

Rita was born in the year of our Lord 1381 and she died in 1456; but her body has not only resisted the processes of nature, but it smells as sweet as roses.

I know this, because the Romanist booklet says so.

The beautiful lie about Rita is thus limpidly related.

Then her former resolve to consecrate herself to God took possession of her and she went to Cascia and sought admittance among the Augustinian Nuns, but her request was refused and she returned to her home in Rocco Porena. Twice more she sought admittance to the convent, then God Himself advocated her cause. In the quiet of her humble home she heard her name called and in a miraculous way she was conducted to the monastic enclosure no entrance having been opened. The nuns, astonished at the miracle, received her and she was soon enrolled among their number. Her hidden and simple life in religion was distinguished by obediance and exactitude. Her penances were extreme. She scourged herself thrice daily. She wore a rough hair shirt and interwoven with her tunic were thorns which from time to time tore her flesh. After listening to a sermon on the Passion she returned to her cell, prostrated herself before her crucifix and begged to feel the pain of at least one of the thorns with which Christ had been crowned. Her prayer was answered and ever afterwards she bore a wound on her forehead so full of corruption and, because of the order she was denied the companionship of her sisters in religion.

The power of miracles was soon recognized with Rita. When the jubilee was proclaimed at Rome by Pope Nicholas IV it was Rita's desire to attend and she was allowed on condition that her wound would be healed, as it was, until she returned. While she was dying she requested a relative to bring her a rose from her old home at Rocca Porena,.and tho it was January, and all roses had ceased to blow, the relative went and found a full grown rose. For this reason roses are blest in her honor. After the death of St. Rita, 1456, her face became radiant in beauty and the odor from her wound was as sweet as the odor of the roses which she loved so well, and it spread all through the convent and into the church, and it remains even to this late day.

Rita was beatified by Pope Urban VIII May 22, 1628. Pope Leo XIII appointed Cardinal Martinelli (formerly Apostolic Delegate to United States) Postulator of Canonization in 1892. The Cardinal visited the Sacred body of Rita and testified as to this supernatural odor, and the proofs were accepted by the congregation of Rites as one of the required miracles. The body has remained incorrupt to this day, and for a time retained its natural color, but at present though changed in appearance, the face is beautiful and well preserved. At her death the lowly cell was aglow with heavenly light and the bells of Cascia were rung by the angels. A relative with a paralyzed arm was cured when the sacred remains were touched. A carpenter who had known the saint expressed a willingness to make her coffin, immediately recovered the use of his stiffened hands."

With what unutterable disgust an intelligent, independent mind contemplates the scoundrels who can make merchandise of such childish fables!

With what pity and wonder, must we witness the mental prostration of the dupes of these cheats and swindlers.

No wonder this foreign church wants to close the mails to exposures of its systematized greed, depravity, and commercialized superstition.

The remainder of the booklet is oc-cupied by forms of prayer to St. Rita, covering the Nine days' debauch. At the close, comes a sort of jig-jingle of prayer-yelps, filling 4 pages, the following being a sample:

Saint Rita, pierced with a thorn,
Saint Rita, deep sea of contrition,
Saint Rita, in ecstasies before the Blessed Sacrament,
O Saint Rita, consumed by divine love,
O Saint Rita, bidden to the bridegroom's throne,
Saint Rita, received in heaven with joy,
Saint Rita, arrayed in unspeakable glory,
Saint Rita, incorrupt in the chaste body,
Saint Rita, advocate of the impossible,
Saint Rita, advocate of desperate cases,
Saint Rita, light of Holy Church,
Saint Rita, cure for the unfaithful,
Saint Rita, sweet balm for every sorrow,
Saint Rita, balsam for every ill,
Saint Rita, persevering in prayers,
Saint Rita, always confident in your prayer,
O Saint Rita, who canst obtain everything from thy dying Jesus,
O Saint Rita, who knows the way to His Sacred Heart,
Saint Rita, our powerful advocate,
Saint Rita, predicted by an angel,
Saint Rita, remarkable in childhood,
Saint Rita, enamored of solitude,
Saint Rita, example of blind obedience,

"Blind obedience!"

Yes, that is the goal for which Rome eternally strives.

"BLIND OBEDIENCE!!!"

Don't read any books but mine!

Don't read anything that tends to uncover *me*.

Don't listen to any sermons but mine!

Don't allow any heretic to tell the truth on *me!*

Close the mails to any accursed non-Romanist who tries to expose my rottenness and my sordid ambition.

In order that you may know how to send in your orders for these miraculous, articles sold by Fitzgerald's church, in Fitzgerald's State, I give you the back-cover advertisement of the booklet. Fitzgerald, you know, is one of the K. of C. Congressmen who wants to close the mails to exposures of Romanism,

1875
The First
Telephone

1916
The Country-wide System

Forty-one Years of Telephone Progress

The faint musical sound of a plucked spring was electrically carried from one room to another and recognized on June 2, 1875. That sound was the birth-cry of the telephone.

The original instrument—the very first telephone in the world—is shown in the picture above.

From this now-historic instrument has been developed an art of profound importance in the world's civilization.

At this anniversary time, the Bell System looks back on forty-one years of scientific achievement and economic progress, and gives this account of its stewardship:

It has provided a system of communication adequate to public needs and sufficiently in advance of existing conditions to meet all private demands or national emergencies.

It has made the telephone the most economical servant of the people for social and commercial intercourse.

It has organized an operating staff loyal to public interests and ideals; and by its policy of service it has won the appreciation and good will of the people.

With these things in mind, the Bell System looks forward with confidence to a future of greater opportunity and greater achievement.

AMERICAN TELEPHONE AND TELEGRAPH COMPANY
AND ASSOCIATED COMPANIES

One Policy   *One System*   *Universal Service*

When the enterprising merchant of Nuremberg, Frederick Hohenzollern, paid the Emperor Sigismund 400,000 gulden for the Marquisate of Brandenburg, he made a good investment. The German people, now pay a yearly interest of much more than a million dollars to the Hohenzollern's on that original investment of $160,000.

When the first German Astor peddled rum for Indian furs, and salted down the profit in Manhattan dirt, he made no better outlay of his money than did Frederick Hohenzollern.

But his descendant, William Hohen-

THE KAISER FOUNTAIN IN CONSTANTINOPLE

zollern—the present Me-and-God egomaniac—also enjoys, during lucid intervals, a commercial venture. For example, he spent several thousand dollars of the money of "my subjects", in erecting a beautiful fountain *in Con-*

stantinople, several years ago. As we have recently learned, the Militarists had even then matured their plans for a great war which was to place the Hohenzollern dynasty where Napoleon aspired to be. A part of the game was, to win the Turks. So, the Kaiser built a fountain in Constantinople, as a delicate compliment to the Sultan and his co-religionists.

The Kaiser visited the Turks, journeyed to Jerusalem, and exhibited his gracious pomposity on a large scale—at the expense of "my subjects."

I wonder that he did not imitate Napoleon to the limit by sitting down, cross-legged, with a turban on his head, and listening intently to the imaums, as they expounded the creed of the Prophet.

However, that fountain was an excellent investment. It tickled the Turks, and inclined their hearts to Herr William Hohenzollern; and, when Armageddon broke loose, there was the infatuated Turk ready to sacrifice himself, to get the Hohenzollern madman out of his scrape. And that is, precisely what the Turk did. He saved the day for the Kaiser, and lost it for himself.

The Kaiser's fountain could have run, night and day, with the blood of the Mohammedans, who have fought and died in the effort to save the ally of the Pope from the ruinous consequences of his own militarist frenzy.

A church which teaches hate, intolerance, and a passion to injure those who honestly reject it, is a deadly danger to Christianity and to the human race.

When such a church incites riots, arson, and murder, it cannot be reconciled with modern ideas and modern progress. Such a church harks back to the Dark Ages.

In the letter below, you will find that a Romanist woman, who probably deludes herself by thinking that she is a Christian, *makes cruel war upon a blind man,* because he sells anti-Romanist literature:

THE AUTHORIZED BLIND MAGAZINE MAN.

Phelan Road, New Rochelle, N. Y.

My Dear Mr. Davis: I have been told that you receive subscriptions to and assist in the circulation of a vile scurrilous paper known as "The Menace." If this is true, I feel reluctantly obliged to take my subscriptions away from you, and influence my friends to do the same. Possibly I have been misinformed, if so I should like to know it.

Yours very truly,

Signed   KATHERINE E. KEOGH.
MRS. MARTIN J. KEOGH.

By the grace of Tammany Hall, the Fitzgerald congressman—who wants Protestant literature put out of the mails—represents a Brooklyn district. The mental condition of the Romanists who elect such a rampant anti-American as Fitzgerald can be learned from a folder just published.

A dollar is angled for in the following persuasive words:

"As only a favored few can have the privilege of being able to visit The Eternal City and so obtain a DIRECT AND PERSONAL BLESSING from the Holy Father, Catholics, far removed, will doubtless be glad to know of a means by which they also can participate in this valued Benediction.

On the opposite page is a quartersize reproduction of the original document, bearing signature and stal of the Holy See, which imparts the Apostolic Benediction, with plenary Indulgence for the honor of death. In it is inserted the full name of the supplicant, and includes all the members of their families. There is a fee charged by the Vatican for the seal and attestation affixed to each blessing which goes towards the maintenance of the Vatican Palaces.

The Blessing is printed on Roman Vellum, with a fine photograph inset, representing His Holiness, BENEDICT XV, seated on Throne and wearing Pontifical Stole, in the act of imparting the Papal Blessing, and round the photograph is a handsome illuminated design bearing the Papal Insignia.

These Blessings, which can be obtained in any language are forwarded by Registered Mail in specially constructed tubes for ample protection.

Remit One Dollar (Express Money Orders accepted)
   to   Miss Josephine Englefield,
     Care American Express Co.
      ROME (Italy)

to cover all expenses, including Apostolic Fee.

Please give full name clearly and unless otherwise stated, Blessings in the English language will be forwarded.

Please do not destroy this, but pass it on to a friend.

The maintenance of the Vatican palaces"! The Vatican proper is a palace containing *eleven thousand rooms*, and 56 grand stair cases, to say nothing of the magnificent gardens, pavilions, etc.

The Pope's income from all sources is not less than three million dollars a year. The revenue from Peter's Pence, alone, never falls below a million. And the money which goes to the Vatican, *stays;* none to speak of ever comes away.

So you see, "the maintenance of the Vatican palaces" requires the sales of many indulgences, blessings, medalions, cords, statues, dispensations and other papal merchandise.

A church which sold Henry VIII. the dispensation to marry his brother's widow, and which so recently sold a divorce to the millionaire Drexels, would sell anything for money—even Christ himself. In fact, they *do* sell and crucify him afresh, in the shocking merchandise they make of all things pertaining to religion.

Shetland Ponies Make Safe Companions

FOR CHILDREN.

Write me for Prices for Well Broken, Well Trained Ponies.

ACCLIMATED. GENTLE. KEEP THEMSELVES.

I AM NOW READY TO SHIP AT A DAY'S NOTICE

50 CHOICE GILTS,

Bred to farrow in March and April from my heaviest, big-litter strains in

Duroc-Jerseys, Poland-Chinas and Berkshires

Will make price on the pick of these gilts of **$50** each. They will weigh about 300 pounds, crated.

JOE J. BATTLE, Box 4, Moultrie, Ga.

Lightning Source UK Ltd.
Milton Keynes UK
UKHW020042260219
337881UK00006B/148/P